MYTH AND LEGEND IN EARLY GREEK ART

MYTH AND LEGEND
IN
EARLY GREEK ART

BY KARL SCHEFOLD

HARRY N. ABRAMS, INC., PUBLISHERS, NEW YORK

Translated by Audrey Hicks
Quotations from the Greek newly translated by Clifford Bartlett

Library of Congress Catalog Card Number: 66-13271

CONTENTS

INTRODUCTION

I wish to proclaim the victor
in the Pythian race of the bronze-shield-bearers,
Telesicrates;
to cry out with the deep-girdled Graces at his triumph—
happy man,
and the glory of Cyrene, the horse-driver.
Once the flowing-haired son of Leto
snatched Cyrene away from the wind-echoing vales of Pelion,
took the huntress-maiden in a golden chariot,
and established her as queen in a fruitful land,
to dwell in plenty at the foundation of a third continent.

PINDAR, *Pyth.* 9, 1–7

The Greeks possessed an immense wealth of legend. The tales were told differently from place to place, changing from generation to generation as they were passed, in ever-varying form, from mouth to mouth. Every noble family traced its descent back to the world of legend in the heroic past; any man who performed a glorious deed would be compared with some legendary hero. Every new occurrence was measured beside myth. In this way the wars of Hellas and Asia were traced back to the Trojan War; the victors in the games could be compared with Heracles and other heroes. Alexander the Great revered Achilles as his ideal.

The legends, however, were no Bible—they were not holy scripture of which every word had been set down and fixed for all time. At each telling the narration of the tales differed giving ever-varying versions in both poetry and art. In giving new forms to the heroic images the Greeks gained a deeper and purer understanding of themselves. Each interpretation of a legend contained, at the same time, an interpretation of its own time. At an early stage Heracles was admired simply as a mighty conqueror of difficulties. A sophisticated civilization made him a lover Pls. 54–62 of music and, later still, his destiny was seen as tragic. Finally he becomes a symbol of redemption since, after all his labours, he is at length admitted into Olympus.

Nowadays, when we think of the past, we think of historical events and personages. The people of antiquity had no interest in fortuitous historical events but endeavoured to grasp that which was truly significant. Where we think of history they thought of legend. Heroes of ancient time were generally imagined as better and stronger than modern men. In face of the greatness of the past the immediately foregoing period, together with the history of contemporary times, appeared of small significance. Not until Classical times did a feeling for history awaken. We shall be able to see this sense of history foreshadowed, at an early stage, in the reshaping of legend, although actual written history is found only after the period *c.* 500 BC.

Of the wealth of legend which existed among the people since prehistoric times only a portion found new form in the historical period of the first millennium; and of the epics, tragedies, paintings and sculptures embodying this new form, again only a portion has survived. However, we are fortunate in possessing lists of the contents of certain lost works as well as fragments of others, and also a rich tradition of painting and sculpture. Many features of legend have survived only in vase-paintings and reliefs; an example of this is the magnificent representation of Pls. 34, 35 the fall of Troy on the relief-decorated amphora from Mykonos; nowhere else are the Wooden Horse and the sufferings of the Trojans depicted in such detail and with such dramatic immediacy.

The illustrations in this book are filled with peculiar motifs, whose specialized and subtle language we shall only gradually learn to understand. They should not be given a mere cursory glance but should be examined as works of art capable of giving ever-increasing pleasure the more closely familiar we become with them. Greek art is never simple illustration; it always has something to say in an individual and particular way. Hellenic legend lives and changes constantly in art no less than in poetry. During the Middle Ages the situation was quite different because there existed a holy scripture which had to be illustrated. The Greeks had no sacred book restricting the scope of their art. The free expression of constant new religious experience was part of the basic content of Greek art.

Anyone wishing to become familiar with the legends will, first of all, read Homer, Hesiod and the tragedians. But visual art is a no less important guide. The enchantment of legend rests in the artistic expression given to it. In many cases, where the written versions of myths have been lost, artistic representations help to bring their content before us. In poems and pictures we can grasp the living legend. Prosaic accounts of the legends, such as we find in handbooks of mythology, are necessary too in that they help us to find our bearings in the world of legend. Yet, whereas the poems describing the anger of Achilles and the homecoming of Odysseus are quite unforgettable and the representations of the deeds of Heracles on the Temple of Zeus in Olympia are profoundly impressive, the tales, as they are retold in the handbooks, slip from the memory. It is strange, moreover, how seldom these handbooks draw on the visual arts as a source of material for they are an inestimable source of living legend. They could become as much a part of our most intimate artistic heritage as are the Biblical illustrations familiar to us from childhood.

The visual arts are an invaluable guide for yet another reason since, from the immeasurable wealth of tradition, they select those aspects which were important to the people of a particular period. Art teaches us to see the legends with the eyes of the Greeks. The various times are characterized by the themes chosen and the artistic form given to them. The illustrated legends bear witness in themselves to the period in which they were created. We must therefore repeatedly ask both what is represented in each period and how it is represented. In not restricting ourselves to a single legend we give ourselves the opportunity to make constant comparisons and to ask why one legend should have been chosen in one particular period and a different one in another as well as why they were conceived in precisely the way they were.

In the early period, for example, there was a greater interest in the conflict among the gods, whilst interest, during the Classical phase, centred on their birth and their amatory activities since the people of the time sought connections and discovered that all things in life are organically and functionally linked. Everything new was linked to mythical archetypes; for every new philosophy of life, artists sought new ways of illustrating the legends. The Greeks' relationship to legend originates in the same spirit of understanding, order and clarity as is found in their philosophy. At the same time, however, new concepts are never compressed within old images, schemes and dogmas: the image of the tradition is constantly changed. The two basic forces in Greek history—tireless progress and a faithful retention of great traditions—come to a compromise in the illustration of myth.

8

It would be artistically dishonest to force certain legends into a connection with one another and to illustrate such connections by means of illustrations drawn from widely divergent periods. Our point of departure should not be the story of the legend but its images. In this book we have attempted, for the first time, to present the largest possible number of Greek illustrations of legends and to show them in their correct relationships both as regards the history of art and the history of thought. We want to learn, as it were, to 'read' the pictures. From time to time it will be necessary to relate the stories in order to elucidate the illustration. The chronological arrangement makes the book, at the same time, a history of Greek narrative style—a study which has not, as yet, been made.

In examining a work of art we have to distinguish three elements: the contents, the form and the composition. As an example we have chosen the plate, now in London, on which Menelaus and Hector are depicted fighting over the fallen Euphorbus. In this case our interpretation of the picture is aided by inscriptions but we will see that these alone are not sufficient to provide full understanding and, in many cases, are even actually misleading. Where there are no inscriptions our only help lies in comparisons with other pictures which have already been interpreted. Such comparisons—even when applied to this apparently straightforward example—reveal an unexpected mystery. It is only through familiarity with a large number of other paintings that we can recognize that the Greek, Menelaus, is to be the victor in this fight since the movement of the victor is generally from left to right. The fallen warrior, however, usually lies on the side of his own party, his feet pointing forward to show that he had been advancing towards the enemy and had not turned to flee. Now Euphorbus, the fallen warrior in this example, was a Trojan; this being so, why is he lying on the side of Menelaus? The answer is that the artist wished to indicate that Menelaus was to have the shield of Euphorbus, and this was in fact still displayed at a later period in the sanctuary of Hera in Argos as a dedicatory offering by Menelaus. The similarity of the decoration on Menelaus' and Euphorbus' shields is also intended to indicate this.

From a question of content we have imperceptibly moved on to one of form or composition. It is apparent that the interpretation of the theme, peculiar to this work, is related to its special form: the two combatants, powerful individual figures, have been singled out from the tumult of the battle together with the fallen warrior. Menelaus is portrayed as somewhat the stronger; the figure of Hector displays less movement but is distinguished by the emblem of an eagle in flight on his shield. The manner in which the pictorial elements are joined on to one another is an archaic trait, whilst the simple power of the forms belongs to the High Archaic phase; the network of gay decoration surrounding the figures is typically eastern Greek. These indications of landscape are, however, at the same time connected with the actual weapon which was felt to be very much a living entity. A spray of volutes and palmettes hangs down into the scene and on either side of its apex is an eye. Eyes are an age-old and widespread motif intended to ward off evil but on Greek pottery they frequently symbolize the life which was felt to reside in the pot. The latter is not dead but flowers in its decoration and looks out at us.

By so describing the contents and the form of the work we gain a clearer understanding of something unique which is given life in such a creation: this is its content or 'inner form.' Only when the actual content reveals itself do we grasp the extratemporal significance of the creation, that which is our most intimate concern and which has had a continuous and productive effect throughout the ages. A mere examination of its contents would not do justice to the character of the work; a mere examination of its form would mean a failure to appreciate that the composition of the contents is an integral part of the form. When the question is regarded in this way the change occurring in legend-illustrations can only be understood through the history of art, and along with the history of poetry it stands as a source in its own right.

In this book we have restricted ourselves to illustrations which are Greek in a strict sense of the word. Were Italic-Greek, Roman and Etruscan legend-illustrations to be similarly treated, a separate book would be required for each subject and these books would be no less illuminating than the present one. The first volume, which presents illustrations from the Early and High Archaic phases, is to be followed by a second one devoted to Late Archaic and Classical works. By its very restriction this book may be of service to the history of Greek literature, art and religion and may show that the illustrations of legend are important evidence of the changes in religious perception and, in fact, of intellectual development in general.

THE PREHISTORY OF LEGEND

Next drank the other leaders. Long-haired Iopas then,
Whom mighty Atlas taught, with golden lyre rings out.
He sings of the journeying moon, the toiling sun,
Whence came the race of men and beasts, whence rain
And fire; of Arcturus he tells, and watery Hyades,
Of the twin bears, and why so fast the winter suns
Haste to the sea, or what holds back the lingering nights.

VIRGIL, *Aeneid* I, 740–46 (F. R. Cowell)

Since men have existed, some highly gifted masters and creators of language have given form, in legends, to archetypal experiences. They have told about the beginning of the world, about the sun and the moon, storms and tides, love and guilt, and the deeds and sufferings of the great. Always men have endeavoured, in their images and cults, to respond to the powers which determine their existence. These primeval myths and customs have provided much which has passed into popular tales.

Early Bronze Age graves on the Greek islands have produced an abundance of carefully worked marble statuettes. Most of these represent women, their heads thrown back, in attitudes suggesting ecstatic movement. But they also include other fortunate dwellers in the higher world of the Dead with a significance evidently the same as that of the later Greek sepulchral terracottas. Those grave-goods, too, in all their diversity, depict a higher world of nymphs and heroes, a world portrayed by artists in ever-varying form yet always retaining its basic character. The strange figures representing flautists, harpists and shawm-players, from those Early Bronze Age graves on the Greek islands, Pl. 1 are reminiscent of shamans, the priests whose activities among certain peoples have been observed up to the present day. By means of magic charms and intoxication the shamans exalt themselves to a visionary state in which they achieve mastery over divine powers. Afterwards they tell of journeys into the Other World from which they bring back precious and sacred spoils. Thus Jason brought back the Golden Fleece and Orpheus went in search of Eurydice. Karl Meuli, who discovered these connections, has also shown that the Orpheus of the Greek legend was Pl. 63a originally one of these magician-minstrels.

The home of Orpheus was traditionally Pieria, the land of the Muses on Mt. Olympus. Later he came to Thrace. Apollo and the Muse Calliope are named as his parents. His wonderful singing brought all creation together in peaceful harmony. Not only animals but also forests, mountains and rivers listened, and even followed his song. When Eurydice, his beloved, died from a snake-bite received as she was fleeing from a rival suitor he descended into Hades where he charmed the ruler and all the inhabitants of the Underworld by his song. He was allowed to lead Eurydice up once more on condition that he should not look back at her on their way to the upper world. When they had climbed almost to the light Orpheus could no longer hear his beloved's step and looked back to

11

see if she were still there, whereupon Hermes led Eurydice back to the Underworld. Thereafter the unhappy man avoided all contact with women but gained such power over the sensibilities of the men of Thrace that their wives grew jealous. In frenzied rage they tore him to pieces during a Dionysiac feast. His head, cast into the river Hebrus, floated down to the sea and then to the island of Lesbos where, still prophesying, it was revered for centuries in an oracle's sanctuary.

In such Greek legends we have a formulation of the ideas foreshadowed in the lays of those early priests, ideas which were dawning and surging in some bold imaginations, in a variety as endless as life itself. By the Late Bronze Age, mythical concepts are becoming clearer, especially on the island of Crete and in the related Mycenaean civilization of the mainland. A minstrel on a rock, the remains of a wall-painting from a Mycenaean palace in Pylos, is similar to the figure of Orpheus and has, in fact, even been identified with him because of the bird above the figure and the fact that he was surrounded by other animals.

Pl. 2b   Figure-compositions of this period are best preserved on seals. On one of these we see nymphs who are bringing sacred lilies to a female figure sitting enthroned under a tree and holding some poppy-stalks. The solemnity of the scene is intensified by the cult-symbol of the double axe together with sun and moon. The lions' heads on the right seem to indicate the ancient custom, interpreted by Meuli, by which the life-containing parts, that is to say the heads or antlers of the slain animals, are given back to the god; for it is not permissible to rob the lords of life of their rightful property. The use of the poppy—a bringer of dreams—may be connected with the mysterious character of the scene. In the distance appears the vision of a god or goddess covered by a large shield. Armed goddesses were worshipped in many places in Greece: the best-known being the city-goddess of Athens. But later phases of Greek art were never again to produce scenes of such a dreamlike quality. On another seal we see a goddess appearing on a mountain and flanked by lions like the later Artemis, Mistress of the Animals. As yet, certainly, there are no actual illustrations of legends as they occur in later Greek art, but the mythical concepts are nevertheless beginning to crystallize. The divinities are no longer simply the actual forces of Nature but are becoming personalized beings, who could become the subjects of legends, although we are still far removed from the clear-cut figures of Classical art.

Figures of nymphs in attitudes suggesting ecstatic movement, of the type found in Early Bronze Age graves on the Greek islands, occur as dedicatory offerings in the sanctuaries of Crete. Many of them are holding snakes in their upraised hands as do the later maenads. In these figures a more definite form is given to the company surrounding the gods. They have been called 'Snake-goddesses' but this is probably incorrect; these beings are not goddesses but belong to an intermediary sphere between men and gods and, as such, could be represented at an earlier date
Pl. 2b   than could the gods themselves. On the gold ring the worshippers who are approaching the seated figure should be interpreted as nymphs rather than mortals.

At first Cretan art, in its representations of sea-creatures and plant-life, gave expression to 'the living robe of divinity' rather than to the divinity itself. Greek artists were the first to make Nature manifest herself in mythical figures—nereids, tritons, maenads and satyrs. The later art of Crete prepares the way for this use of definite figures in the first place in its clearer vision of divinity. During the last few years some Mycenaean sanctuaries, such as the small city-temple on the island of Ceos, have produced fragments of cult-images some of which must have been life-size. The house of a god worshipped in a cult is part of his anthropomorphic manifestation and thus we find, at Eleusis as in other Mycenaean holy places, a rectangular structure with a pronaos and this is the prototype of the Greek temple. This prelude to the later Greek worship of anthropomorphic gods is all the more remarkable in

12

that, except for figurines, as far as we know the gods were portrayed only on stone pillars and on plaques during the Geometric period, *i.e.* the period *c.* 1000 BC, following that of the Mycenaean civilization.

Historical events are another important root of mythology. In the chief places where legends are localized, Mycenaean cities and other remains have been discovered: Heracles is the lord of Tiryns, a city which, through the excavations of Schliemann, has become no less famous than Mycenae. Minos rules in Crete where the Athenian Theseus overcomes the bull-headed man, the Minotaur. In Argos we find Adrastus, who is commander in the war of the Seven against Thebes. The Argonauts, when they set out to win the Golden Fleece, start from Iolcus in Thessaly. They were originally Minyans from Boeotian Orchomenus where a particularly fine tholos tomb has been preserved. From Aphidnae in Attica comes Theseus, the first abductor of Helen; the Dioscuri, who bring home their ravished sister, come from Sparta; from Troy comes Paris, and no sooner has Helen been married to Menelaus, King of Sparta, than he steals her away again. But this time a greater undertaking is necessary to win her back: Menelaus' brother, Agamemnon, King of Mycenae, leads the united Greeks on a campaign of revenge on the Trojans. The table and the map on p. 182 show other correspondences between archaeological sites and the places in which legends are localized.

> But when earth had covered   this generation
> Zeus son of Cronus   made another, the fourth
> on the fruitful earth   better and nobler,
> a godlike race   half-gods by name,
> the race before ours   on the fertile earth.
> Some were destroyed   by murdering war
> at seven-gated Thebes   the land of Cadmus,
> as they fought   over the flocks of Oedipus;
> others when they sailed   over the sea
> to distant Troy   for flowing-haired Helen;
> death was the end   that overshadowed them.
> But to others Father Zeus   son of Cronus
> gave a living and a home   far from men
> at the end of the world.   There they dwell
> untouched by sorrow   by the deep-swirling ocean,
> contented heroes   in the isles of the blest.
> Three times a year   the grain-giving earth
> bears honey-sweet fruit.   Far from the gods,
> Cronus rules over them . . .

HESIOD, *Works and Days*, 156–73

The core of historical truth in the legends must have come down to us through heroic lays as they were then composed. In artistic character these poems must have corresponded to the mighty cities of the kings and the tholos tombs of their ancestors who were worshipped as heroes. Certain isolated representations, such as the delicate silver relief showing an attack on a city by the sea, can also give us some idea of this type of poetry. In describing his deeds Pl. 2a

13

the poets were attempting to capture and comprehend the mysterious and superhuman strength of the ruler, the hero. They must have possessed the courage to go beyond the mere description of glory and greatness, as is the practice with other peoples, and to go on to describe curses and sacrilege in the lives of the heroes revered as super-human beings. For the sake of the Trojan campaign, Agamemnon sacrifices his daughter Iphigenia. For this act he

is slain, on his return, by his unfaithful wife; his son Orestes later kills his own mother as an act of atonement. Boldness in portraying the horror of such reality acquires its greatest profundity in Classical tragedy. The fate of the hero embraces the greatness and tragedy of god-given existence. From the cult of the hero to that of the god Dionysus, celebrated in tragedy, is a direct path; Dionysiac exaltation opens the mind to visions of heroic destiny.

When the first Greek tribes migrated to Hellas shortly after 2000 BC they must certainly have brought with them some of their own legends and these we may call 'primeval' myths. In their new homes these myths were supplement-ed by the immeasurably richer tales which they learned from ancient Mediterranean peoples, among whom the inhabitants of the Greek islands stand out as exceptionally gifted. The Greeks gained a clearer conception of the Great Goddess, Mistress of Life, in her various manifestations: as Hera in her role of consort to Zeus, Lord of the Heavens; then also as Demeter, Mother Earth, and Aphrodite who enjoys her lover Adonis, loses him and then wins him back again. In other places she was manifest as Athene whose armed state is an expression of the immense power of divinity (Aphrodite and other goddesses can also appear armed); in yet other places she appears as Leto, mother of the twins Apollo and Artemis. She could also be worshipped as Meter, the Universal Mother. The Great Goddess could even be manifest in Artemis herself.

Apollo and Zeus are both originally children of the Great Goddess: Apollo is the son of Leto, and Zeus, in Crete, is the son of the Great Mother. By the second millennium, however, both have already become mightier than their mothers; a father-religion replaces the mother-religion. And so, with slowly increasing clarity, the company of the gods takes shape. The differentiation of mythical figures becomes even more clearly comprehensible in the first millennium; but even in the early period the variety of legends must have been great enough to afford a correspond-ence between the world of the spirit and the wealth of forms encountered in the external world.

THE CHRONOLOGY OF THE LEGENDS

In the twelfth century BC the Doric Greeks immigrated into Hellas and destroyed the Mycenaean civilization. Some of the pre-Doric population emigrated to the islands and to Asia Minor where they became known as Ionians and Aeolians. This period of political upheaval brought about an intrinsic change in the characters both of the original population and of the immigrants who, in the state of fruitful tension which resulted from their proximity, were mutually influential. This change is most apparent in the creation of the Geometric Style in Athens, the first phase Pls. 3a, b of which is known as the 'Protogeometric.' The visionary outlook of Cretan and Mycenaean artists, together with a rather gentle perception of Nature, is replaced by an austere type of art restricted to economical forms yet expressive of confidence in a cosmos, in an order conceived as ordered by the god, Apollo. Diverse ornaments and images were brought together to form a totality rich in associations; basic rhythms and archetypal images of life were made visible. The importance of the Protogeometric and Geometric phases can be assessed from the fact that, together, they span a third of the history of Greek art, approximately three centuries (1000–700 BC) out of nine (1000–100 BC).

Behind the new style lay a completely unprecedented conception of divine form, order and power. Then, for the first time, the Olympian gods must have been seen as a family in which each member had his or her particular sphere of power but in which all were subject to Zeus as their lord and king. According to Herodotus this view goes back to Homer and Hesiod and it is true that these poets had a strong influence on the imagination for thousands of years. But Homer assumes that the family of the Olympians is already familiar to his hearers (cf. genealogical table, p. 183): Hera holds sway as the consort of Zeus; Poseidon rules over the sea and Hades over the Underworld; Apollo is the patron of the Muses, Hephaestus god of sculptors, Athene goddess of intelligent warfare and Ares god of savage and murderous slaughter; Hermes is the messenger of the gods; Artemis belongs to the open air, to wild life and the hunt whilst Demeter is goddess of the fruits of the field; Aphrodite works her enchantment in love and in life. This magnificently simple conception of the distribution of divine power now seems all too familiar. It was one of the most significant steps taken along the path of human intellectual progress, comparable to the creation of Geometric art and, with this, of Greek art proper. At an earlier date each divinity was manifest as an independent power. The only relationships recognized were those between mother and son and goddess and consort. Some great poet of the Geometric period must have been the first to envisage the Olympian family with the boldly differentiated characteristics indicated here; these characterizations find their most mature expression in the east frieze of the Parthenon. But even in archaic illustrations of legends we see solemn processions of the company of the Olympians Fig. 5 in which the figures are already clearly differentiated. Pls. 10, 48a

In actual cults each god's authority and power continue to be more all-embracing than would appear from the family arrangement outlined above. In the locality of his cult a god was revered as an omnipotent ruler in which form he had frequently been worshipped even in Mycenaean times. Thus in Argos the goddess Hera was an all-embracing power, far more than the mere consort of Zeus; in the same way, even today in many places, the faithful offer all their devotion to the Virgin Mary, Queen of Heaven. It seems that Zeus did not enter into his dominion over Olympia and Dodona until after the Doric migration, whereas the cult of Poseidon on the isthmus of Corinth may well be older. At all events the cults of Apollo and Athene in Delphi, of Leto and her children Apollo and Artemis on Delos, of Hera in Argos, of Athene in Athens and of Demeter in Eleusis are all Mycenaean. In each of these places the god or goddess in question was the sole object of worship. But the Greeks, with their philosophical outlook, sought an order behind the diversity of these cults just as in art, from the Geometric period onwards, they sought the archetypal images within the diversity of life. Thus out of the many autonomous divinities, legend created a family in which each member had his or her own function taking its place within the whole.

The fact that, after the stormy interlude of the Doric migration, people of widely differing origin found themselves living together in their new homes, aided the shaping of mythical traditions. Everyone knew the tales told about his own gods and now he could find, as he encountered the new divinities, related traits as well as characteristics of a surprising strangeness. Great poets, whose names we no longer know, elucidated this experience for the immigrants, and then for all Greeks, in the vision of the family of the Olympians. At the same time this new outlook gave the Greeks a sense of possessing a common religion and nationality.

The heroic sagas underwent a similar process. The lays which had been recited in honour of heroes of the time in the native lands of the immigrants now moved away into a distant past. The need awoke to create a coherent whole from the abundance of traditional material. It may be that men of an earlier period had sung of the king of Mycenae and of his campaign against Troy. But now the greatest possible number of heroes are given a part in this campaign which, in the epic poetry of the subsequent centuries, is gradually made into a continuous narrative covering events from the creation of the world to the migration of the Dorians. The endless variety of local poems (hymns) were brought together to form cycles and family trees; they were, in fact, put into a system which suited the logical and historically conscious Greek mind. This capacity to see things as a whole, which continued to be developed throughout many centuries culminating in Hellenism, was an achievement which cannot command enough admiration. In it the Hellenic national consciousness and the Hellenic character found an expression as original as the Geometric style in art with its tendency to organize, arrange, divide up and animate its motifs. But more important than all this was the ability to see the gods as personalized figures, an outlook which completely ousted the ecstatic nature-religion. Although the development of the cyclic sequence of legends may have taken centuries, that one great event, the actual acquirement of a personalized vision of divinity, is already present from the beginning of Geometric art and thus of Greek art (cf. below, p. 28).

Legend is silent on the subject of any political changes following the Doric migration. It is remarkable that the events after the Doric migration did not give rise to any myths of their own, since the tales of even later happenings were, for long afterwards, interwoven with fabulous features: we might consider, for instance, the tales of Homer or the Seven Wise Men (see below, p. 51). But this type of storytelling differs completely from the manner in which the material of the old legends was treated. The ancient legends, in their new artistic form, were deliberately opposed to the historical past. The themes remained those of the primeval myths and the heroic lays. The Mycenaean civilization was still remembered as a better age, a heroic age, whereas the period after the Doric migration was felt to be less favoured, an age of iron. At first therefore only the descendants of the Mycenaeans, and not the newly immigrant Dorians, were able to think of the mythical past; so it is no wonder that our earliest epics, those of Homer, are based on Aeolian-Ionian traditions. The logical and philosophical revelation of a legendary world is an incomparable achievement of the Ionian Greeks; it exists among no other people.

The genealogical table on p. 183 and the table on p. 182 should help us to grasp the main connections between the

16

legends. At the beginning there exist four generations of gods: Mother Earth (Gaea) and her consort the Sky (Uranus) beget Cronus and the other Titans. Cronus fathers Zeus and his Olympian brothers and sisters on Rhea. From Zeus are descended the younger Olympians and countless heroic families. But the overlordship of the king of the gods does not remain undisputed. Typhon, a monster of many shapes, together with the Giants, is borne by Mother Earth to combat Zeus; even the Titans, the older generation of the gods, rise up against him (cf. p. 53).

The legend of the interchange and strife between the generations of the gods originated in the East; it is evidence of a profound realization of the instability of earthly powers. The legend was probably borrowed from the East in Mycenaean times and then given its own peculiar inflection. One concept, at any rate, which is typically Greek is seen in the fact that all the antagonists are descended from the same mother, the Earth, whose children also include men. Thus the ancient oriental dualism, which divided the world into a light and a dark side, collapses.

According to an oracle Zeus was to father a son on Metis, daughter of the sea-god Oceanus, and this son would cause his downfall. Zeus' swallowing of Metis and the subsequent birth of the child with which she was pregnant from his head would seem to be a Greek version of the ancient doctrine of the ages of the world, for Metis means 'wisdom' ('counsel' according to Robert Graves): word and legend are inseparable from the Greek image of Zeus and his intelligent daughter Athene. The idea of Athene's birth from the head of Zeus is actually impossible to represent in art and must therefore belong to a time in which any desire to represent such a story artistically was still quite remote. The legend of the birth of the goddess, fully-armed, from the head of Zeus is more appropriate to the masculine character of the Mycenaean Greeks than to the matriarchal Cretan civilization. So here we may possibly grasp the origins of one of the individual myths which were fitted into the great connected whole of mythology as created in the Geometric period.

Heroic and human families are also linked with divine lineages. Under the Titans the world enjoyed the happy age of gold; the ages of silver and bronze followed under the Olympians to be finally succeeded by our generation of iron which is the farthest removed from the gods. There are other peoples who measure their own times beside the example of their ancestors. But the pessimistic note in this new interpretation of the ancient doctrine of the ages of the world is profoundly Greek. It also contains a moral stimulus in the idea that the better we remember the time when men were still close to the gods, the nearer we are to them ourselves. Mnemosyne, the high Titaness whose name means 'memory,' was the mistress of Zeus and, by him, became mother of the Muses; to them we owe the true poetical life.

When poets of the Geometric period looked for an order and a coherence within the diversity of heroic legend they could begin with the local traditions which must certainly have already contained some genealogical connections: as for instance in Agamemnon as son of Atreus and father of Orestes. As the Trojan War came to be a common war of the Greeks, the heroes from different regions who took part became contemporaries. In this way the stories acquired lineages of heroes. At a later date, in about the sixth century, the sequence of the generations was conceived as it is shown, in simplified form, in the table on p. 182. The first row of heroes are the lovers, friends or children of gods: heroes of this type include Hyacinthus the minion of Apollo, Pelops the minion of Poseidon and his adversary Oenomaus; Aeacus the son of Zeus; Cadmus the consort of the divine Harmonia and Cecrops the first king of Attica who was born of the Earth.

The following generation is that of the powerful slayers of monsters: Perseus who dared to cut off the head of the terrible Medusa; and Bellerophon who conquered the Chimaera, a hybrid creature part lion, part serpent and part fire-breathing goat. We have placed Laius with them, simply because he is the father of Oedipus who brings us to

17

the next generation. Here, for the first time, we find one of those typical Greek enterprises in which many famous heroes take part: the expedition of the Argonauts to Colchis where their leader, Jason, wins the Golden Fleece. Like their fathers, the heroes of this generation also slay monsters but now the interest is centred not on the deed itself but on the fate of the hero. It may be that he distinguishes himself by the number of marvellous deeds he performs, like Heracles and Theseus; or the extraordinary feature may be the number of those taking part in his enterprises as is the case with Jason and the Argonauts and with Meleager and the Hunt of the Calydonian Boar. It may even be that he shocks by the monstrousness of his personal fate as is the case with Oedipus. King Minos of Crete, a figure who appears to be of an earlier character, belongs to this generation as the enemy of Theseus, as does Telamon the helper of Heracles.

After the Calydonian Hunt and the voyage of the Argonauts we have a third joint undertaking, that of the 'Seven against Thebes,' the first battle for a city. In our table we find Adrastus, the leader of the expedition, and Tydeus, one of the most barbarous of the combatants. All the attackers succumbed. Amphiaraus, the pious seer who had already taken part in the Calydonian Hunt and the expedition of the Argonauts, vanished into the earth and became a god of healing. To what extent the Calydonian Hunt, the expedition of the Argonauts and the battle of the seven heroes against Thebes were consciously linked in the Geometric period we do not know; in the visual arts these connections do not become apparent until *c.* 600 BC but then they acquire all the greater significance.

The most far-reaching connections of all are brought together in the fourth and most famous of the heroic expeditions, the Trojan War. We can say with certainty that this cycle of legends had already been formulated in Geometric times because the oldest parts of the Homeric poems—the lay of the Wrath of Achilles and the Homeward Voyage of Odysseus—depend on it for their material. From the whole history of the Trojan War, Homer picks out only those events which lead to the Wrath of Achilles, and its consequences. For ten years the Greeks have besieged Troy without any visible success and now, in the tenth year, events seem to be taking a turn for the worse. Agamemnon has offended Chryses, the priest of Apollo, by keeping Chryseis, daughter of the priest, as his share of the booty from a plundering expedition. Therefore Apollo sends a plague on the camp and Agamemnon is forced to return Chryseis in atonement to the god and his priest. As recompense Agamemnon takes for himself Briseis, Achilles' beloved slave-girl, which action arouses such passionate anger in Achilles that he refuses to take any further part in the war. But without Achilles, their most glorious hero, the Greeks are sorely pressed. In the emergency Achilles' friend Patroclus puts on the divine armour of Achilles and joins the fray. The Trojans flee before the supposed Achilles but are soon aware of the deception and withstand Patroclus who falls in the battle. The inconsolable Achilles is given new weapons by his divine mother and then takes a terrible revenge on the Trojans slaying Hector, the shield and protector of the city.

Fig. 36

> Sing, Goddess,   the wrath of Achilles,
> that murderous wrath   of the son of Peleus
> which cast suffering   upon countless Achaeans
> and sent mighty heroes   to the house of Hades,
> their bodies carrion   for the dogs and birds,
> for thus Zeus willed—   sing from where first
> sprang the disunity   of the son of Atreus,
> Agamemnon,   and godlike Achilles.
>
> *Iliad* I, 1–7

Every aspect of this narrative betrays a great poet with a new and deep insight into the human heart. Never before had men seen the passion of kings, the wounded love of the hero, the loyalty of the friend and the solitary grandeur of the last warrior-hero, Hector, whose fall is also the fall of the city. We shall find a related nobility of vision in the visual arts *c.* 700 BC and this not merely in scenes of Troy. Homer's poems bear witness to the pre-existence of comprehensive, condensed narratives of Greek legends. The number of themes taken from legend which are attested by visual art from the years *c.* 700 BC is so great that we can have no doubt of the great range of those tales. We know nothing of their literary form. But there must have been poets of genius before Homer as significant for the heroic legends as those whom we have seen already had been for the legends of the gods: they sorted out and combined the great wealth of themes.

One such poet gave the Trojan War those far-reaching connections which were Homer's heritage. That poet did not inquire into the intimate emotions of the heroes as Homer does, but we can nevertheless credit him with some splendid creations. Helen, miracle among women, as the cause of the war; Achilles, miracle among men, gives it its brightest lustre. Achilles is contrasted with Paris, Helen's abductor, and with Hector, hero of the Trojans. Other figures whom we may recognize beside Achilles are the mighty hero Ajax who suffers a dismal fate, and Odysseus who endures infinite travail. The only way of seeing the connections between all these great figures is by recounting the legend as it appeared to later periods.

Three goddesses, Hera, Athene and Aphrodite, quarrel over which of them is the fairest. To settle the matter they summon, as judge, Paris the handsome son of the Trojan king whilst he is tending his flock in the isolation of Mount Ida. Paris decides in favour of Aphrodite and, as a reward, receives the most glorious of women, Helen, wife of King Menelaus of Sparta. Paris succeeds in abducting Helen but Menelaus, together with his brother Agamemnon, King of Mycenae, musters all the heroes of Greece to take part in the campaign of revenge. It is of the greatest importance to win to the cause Achilles, son of Peleus and the ocean-goddess Thetis. Zeus himself had been in love with Thetis but he had been told of a prophecy—one of those with which we are already familiar (cf. p. 17) giving warning of a threat to his overlordship—that the son of Thetis would become stronger than his father. So Peleus, who had already distinguished himself in the Calydonian Hunt and as one of the Argonauts, experienced the wonderful happiness of marriage to an immortal and all the gods came with gifts to his wedding. His son Achilles is reared by a divine being, the wise Centaur Cheiron, who had already been the guardian of many heroes including Jason. Thetis knows that her son will prefer an early and glorious death to a long, inglorious life. Her efforts to make him invulnerable when still a baby had proved to be vain; his 'Achilles heel' remained vulnerable and here he will later be struck by Paris' arrow. In vain also Thetis has Achilles brought up on the island of Scyros among the daughters of King Lycomedes: the cunning Odysseus brings the girls a gift of jewellery but he hides some weapons among the trinkets. Achilles notices the hidden objects which attract him more than the jewellery and is thus revealed as the young hero.

Actual motifs in these tales could be older; but the manner in which they are combined betrays the poet who was the forerunner of Homer. It is this way of thinking which gradually makes the tapestry of legend—from the origin of the world to the Doric migration—into a connected sequence as shown by our table (p. 182). If we now turn to the family trees (pp.183–86) it is apparent that the sequence of generations in many cases does not agree with that given in our table. Thus we find (p. 183) Bellerophon in the same generation as Jason and Nestor although he really belongs to an earlier one, and so on. From this we can see that the poets of the Archaic phase, who established these connections, possessed set sequences of the generations which still continued to be handed down.

Pl. 5c
Fig. 13

Pl. 48a

The family trees also contain elements which we owe to later epics or even to the scholars of Classical and Hellenistic times. Thus (on p. 183) we find Hellen (from whom the name 'Hellenes' is derived) as daughter of Deucalion and Pyrrha, the parents of the human race. Hellen's sons are Aeolus, founder of the Aeolian race, Dorus, founder of the Dorian race, and Xuthus from whom the Achaeans and Ionians are descended. It is clear that this genealogy presupposes the subdivision of the Greek tribes after the Doric migration and it is worth noting how large a number of heroes are descended from Aeolus alone. These are, in particular, the heroes of the legends of the Calydonian Hunt, the journey of the Argonauts and the war of the Seven against Thebes. It could be that this particular family tree goes back to an epic composed *c*. 600 BC, a time at which this group of legends, as we will see, is beginning to have a great influence on the visual arts. Similarly the family tree on p. 184, in the centre of which stands the name of Oedipus, corresponds to a Theban epic going back to quite different roots. We should seek these not in the Greek past but in the East with all its wonders, in Egypt where the Greeks rediscovered their Io of the cow's horns in the great goddess Isis; we should also seek them in Phoenicia, the home of Europa and of the alphabet which Cadmus brought to the Greeks. Other family trees—those of the Tantalids, of Achilles and of the Trojan royal family—must stem from the great poets of the Geometric period since their pre-existence is already attested by Homer.

Thus he spoke,   but Achilles was stirred,
his mind in doubt   whether to draw his sword,
press through the crowd   and kill Agamemnon,
or check his passion,   smother his pride.
While thus his mind   wavered within him,
his long sword   half-unsheathed,
the Goddess Athene   appeared from heaven
(sent by the will   of white-armed Hera,
who loved them both   and for both was anxious).
She stood behind   and seized Achilles
by his golden hair;   he alone saw her
(those standing by   saw no one).
But Achilles turned,   looked in amazement,
knew at once   Pallas Athene.

Iliad I, 188–200

Homer has a new view of the hero, seeing not merely his deeds and sufferings but also the daemonic passion determining his actions. Something of the intrinsic grandeur of his heroic figures is also found in Late Geometric bronzes and paintings (cf. especially Pls. 4a and 7b). In the opinion of E. Buschor a bronze group in New York represents Zeus in combat with one of those antagonists whom he must overcome in order to wrest his dominion and establish Pl. 4a it over the Olympians. It has been possible to back this interpretation by a rather later version of the same theme in which the victor is wielding the thunderbolt. Hesiod, in the *Theogony*, describes three such victories of Zeus. We Fig. 4 meet his victory over the Titans in the Corfu gable, and his conquest of the Giants is illustrated on vases from the Fig. 16, Pl. 43 mid-sixth century onwards. In these battles Zeus has to contend with several antagonists of human form but the victory over Typhon is described by Hesiod as a duel with a serpent-like monster of many shapes. In early art such monsters are sometimes depicted as Centaurs; even Medusa, on one Early Archaic relief-decorated amphora, is Pl. 15b given this form to express the greatest extreme of horror. The fact that Zeus' antagonist in the New York group is one of these hybrid creatures seems to confirm his identification as Typhon.

In comparison with contemporary poetry, the expression appears surprisingly restrained. Only the swelling of the calves and the strain apparent in the positions of the heads stand opposed, as it were, to the Geometric pattern to which the artist is trying to keep. Yet artists like the one who produced this group established a new outlook. Our early bronzesmith was one of the first to venture to depict the dominion of Zeus by means of one of his victorious encounters with an antagonist, a device which is to be used for centuries so that Zeus comes to be seen as a warrior

21

or thunderbolt-wielder. But even more surprising is the contrast to what has gone before. The Geometric period had depicted only situations of life of the type used by Homer for his images: animals and their encounters, funeral feasts, dances, contests, processions and battles on land and sea. This representation of the duel with Typhon is, to our knowledge, the first instance of an individual scene from a legend replacing a Geometric archetypal image. Such a work contains a new religious feeling of closeness to the gods; in struggling to reproduce their image men are giving form to their own life.

Pl. 3

The first of the heroes that we meet is Heracles, the most popular of the warrior-heroes. Countless oral tales about him must have been current. In the Archaic period he is already the subject of many poems and in Classical times of high tragedies. But he was never to find a poet who could glorify him in as pure and clear a light as Homer glorified Achilles. Yet he was a son of Zeus and became one of the Olympian gods after his death; he was even allowed to marry Hebe, the lovely daughter of Zeus and Hera. Nevertheless at the same time the character and fate of this man of strength contained ludicrous elements which, at a later period, much occupied writers of comedy.

Even in the story of his birth, monstrous features are combined with comic ones. Zeus falls in love with Alcmene, wife of Amphitryon, King of Thebes. In order to come to her undisturbed and to deceive the jealous Hera he puts on the shape of Amphitryon whilst the real husband is away at war. The ruler of worlds lengthens the duration of one night to three, remaining all this time with Alcmene and conceiving with her the man who is to be the most accomplished of all creation. The night before Alcmene's confinement he boasts that this day a man will be born who is to be mightier than all other men and all sons of Zeus. After making Zeus confirm this with an oath Hera tries to thwart his plan by hastening the birth of Eurystheus; later, as king of the realm of Argos, he is to rule over countless men and then even Heracles, the son of Zeus, will have to serve him. Thus Zeus' oath was to be fulfilled quite differently from the way he had intended. Hera even tries to hinder Alcmene's delivery by making Eleithyia, goddess of childbirth, sit with locked hands beside the unfortunate Alcmene. But suddenly a weasel runs by, Eleithyia raises her hands in fright and Alcmene is delivered.

For the present we will relate no more of the legend and move on via the pictures to the vicissitudes of Heracles' life. It was necessary to say something about the hero's mysterious origins because very little of the story of his birth has been preserved in art; even the short account given here has already characterized the individuality of the Heracles-legend. It embraces the whole of life, from its lighter elements to its deepest mysteries. Later Zeus is finally to come into his own: Heracles is indeed forced to serve Eurystheus, the protégé of Hera, but eventually, after all his travail, he is accepted among the gods: a bold and portentous symbol of human destiny in general, caught between earthly entanglements and divine predestination.

Pl. 4b

Bronze tripods were the finest dedicatory gifts offered in the Geometric period. The leg of one of these tripods, from Olympia, shows two helmeted heroes in combat over a tripod whilst, in a neighbouring scene, we see two lions fighting—this is a Homeric image for the savagery of the heroes. One of Heracles' boldest acts was to penetrate the sanctuary of Apollo in Delphi in order to steal the tripod from which Apollo's oracle, the Pythia, prophesied. But he was opposed by Apollo himself, the only antagonist to whom Heracles ever succumbed. It fits in with the grand Archaic attitude to the figure of Heracles that, in the very first portrayal of him that we encounter, he is measuring himself beside a god who, like himself, is a son of Zeus. But he is unable to shatter the divine order which is, rather, made firmer by Apollo's victory as it is by Zeus' victory over Typhon.

Pl. 4a

To a greater extent than in the type-images, gestures are freed from the restriction of the Geometric pattern, and the daemonic grandeur of the heroes becomes more clearly visible. In the same way it is possible to observe the

22

shift towards a type of passionate expressionism in other spheres in the Late Geometric period from 750 to 700 BC. The extraordinarily large number of Heraclean scenes from the decades *c.* 700 BC seem to suggest that, at this time, the first definite poems about the deeds of Heracles were being composed. We find representations of the particular deeds which, at a later date, were always shown as the first: we see him fighting with the Nemean lion whose skin Pl. 5a he afterwards wears in place of a cloak and cuirass. Then we see him cutting off the heads of the fire-breathing Hydra, the stumps of which he, or his friend Iolaus, must sear in order to prevent their sprouting again; and we see him catching the wonderful hind (cf. p. 195).

In the mysterious early painting of the fight with the Hydra the episode is not yet related with the compactness Pl. 6a and concentration of the Heraclean scenes we have looked at already. Rather timidly and gropingly, but with a wonderful delicacy, the elements of the story are put together; it is almost as though they are of account only when placed in relation with the mighty image of life, the rosette. The Wooden Horse on the right of the picture will be discussed later. At present we must look to the left of the picture at the gigantic Hydra-serpent with its six heads and at the elongated figure of the hero as he clasps the Hydra around the neck and holds his sword in his right hand. It is unfortunate that the chest and head have been broken off, but the hugeness of his stature can be assessed by comparison with the figure of his companion Iolaus at the bottom of the picture: Iolaus, who would appear to be of normal stature, is trying to saw through the body of the serpent with a toothed sickle. To the left of the scene a giant crab tries to bite Heracles' legs and all around there are fishes and birds to indicate the perilous swamp in which the Hydra lives.

Another of Heracles' beneficent deeds is recalled by the shoulder-painting on a Late Geometric oinochoe: the Pl. 5b lake of Stymphalus at the foot of Mount Cyllene was ill-famed on account of the terrible birds which nested there. Their feathers were as sharp as arrows and wounded anyone who came near; it was even said that they ate men. By means of a rattle Heracles frightened the birds out of the bushes on the river-bank in which they were hiding, after which they could not escape the sure aim of his arrows. In our illustration we see a man grasping by the neck one of the many agitated birds and throttling it. This figure could well be Heracles whose battle with these dangerous creatures must surely have contained elements other than those which have chanced to be handed down in writing. Thus, on a metope in the Temple of Zeus in Olympia, we see Heracles bringing slain birds to his protectress Athene and here too he is clasping the birds around the neck. At all events, the illustration stands out from the typical Geometric vases as an unusual scene demanding a particular explanation, as do the other early attempts to portray legends in pictures.

In Late Geometric art we find many double-bodied monsters, such as the Moliones, sons of Poseidon (their mortal father was Actor), the enemies of Heracles and victors of the youthful Nestor. They invaded Pylos with many companions and war-chariots whilst Nestor, without the knowledge or consent of his father and when still little more than a boy, had set out to meet them alone and chariotless. We see him in the centre of the frieze boldly Pl. 7a attacking, with sword and spear, the huge double-bodied creature.

The more austere composition of the bronze fibula was produced in the Early Archaic period. On it we see Pl. 6b Heracles charging full tilt from the left, bearing sword and spear, to do battle with both weapons against the huge double giant who, although armed with three spears, stands as though rooted to the spot: this double giant must be the offspring of Moliona and Poseidon, 'born with the white horses from a silver egg' as the poet Ibycus describes them (Fragment 2).

Besides those deeds of Heracles, which were only single episodes, concerned with single monsters, the Late

Geometric period was already familiar with another deed which meant a tragic doom for the hero. Heracles was so violently in love with Deianeira, daughter of King Oeneus of Calydon, that he succeeded in overcoming her suitor, the venerable river-god Achelous, although the latter was able to turn himself into any shape and was thus almost invincible. But Heracles managed to break Achelous' power by snapping the horn on his head. Later this horn was Pl. 58b thought to be the cornucopia of Amaltheia which automatically filled with every kind of food and drink that the possessor desired.

Having won Deianeira for his wife by overcoming Achelous, Heracles wished to take her to his own home but, to do so, they had to cross the River Evenus which had filled its broad bed with flood-waters. The Centaur Nessus, who was roaming the river-valley, offered to carry Deianeira across whilst Heracles swam. There is a Geometric Pl. 6c gem which shows Nessus dragging a woman along by the hand; she is very slightly built and is wearing a long robe. One of her arms is raised and she seems to be lamenting because, according to the legend, Nessus, true to his Centaur's nature, tried to violate her. The river landscape is suggested by a large water-bird together with a few forceful decorative motifs. The contrast between the great Centaur with his expansive gestures and hairy upraised head and the delicate, defenceless bride gives this little scene an unforgettable grandeur of expression. An observer knows that Nessus is to be fatally wounded by Heracles' arrow and that, as he dies, the Centaur will advise Deianeira to save some of the blood from his wound and to smear Heracles' garment with it if ever his love should fail.

One Early Archaic fragment shows this arrow-shot of Heracles but more frequently we see Heracles in the act Pl. 59 of striking Nessus dead. Artists have shown a preference for this motif because it better expresses Heracles' strength and the passionate rage of his jealousy. Centaurs are not only monsters but can also be venerable beings. One Centaur, Cheiron, was a famous educator of heroes on Mount Pelion: his charges, at one time or another, included Jason and Achilles. Nessus, in his deception and forcing of Deianeira, is merely acting in accordance with the incalculably daemonic element in Nature.

We shall discover later how the passion of Heracles is to be his doom in the same way as the anger of Achilles brings misfortune upon the Greeks and upon himself. Our illustration, together with numerous Archaic representations of the hero in which such associations occur, leads to the supposition that there was already a poem about Heracles in the Homeric period and that this poem did not restrict itself to the simple narration of his deeds, but had a more profound understanding of the hero: as one who loved passionately and was destroyed by his passion. In this type of Homeric poem the deeds are not described in simple succession but are placed in a logical relationship and developed from the character of the hero. Sophocles' tragedy, *The Trachinian Women*, is based on some such ancient poem.

The daemonic grandeur of the hero is apparent in a painting with a different theme to which we will now turn. Pl. 7b The most powerful of the early representations of Heracles is on a clay shield discovered by E. Kunze which had been dedicated to the sanctuary of Hera in Tiryns; it is the earliest surviving monumental painting in Greek art. Its identification with Heracles is confirmed by a slightly later painting of the same type in which the names of Heracles and his companion Iolaus, as well as those of the Amazon queen Andromache and her helpers, have been added. The stature and the actions of the heroes, with their expansive gestures and passion-filled eyes, characterize them as daemonic beings. The differences in stature, in weapons and in clothing seem to compress and concentrate the effect of the scene; there is a tremendous gradation from the figure of the fallen Amazon at the bottom of the picture to the bird announcing doom to the Amazons and, finally, the enormous plume in the helmet of the conqueror. The scene lacks the Archaic tectonics which would make it fully monumental, that is to say a construction

24

1   Abduction of Helen (?). Pithos from Knossos. Height 45.7 cm. (18 in.). *c.* 700 BC.—Heraclion

based on firm supporting surfaces and bodies. The figures speak through their expressively extended limbs; their bodies do not, as yet, possess a firm unity. But the greater solidity of Archaic art causes the loss of that strange expressiveness which is peculiar only to such Late Geometric works. One version of the legend, belonging to a later tradition, tells how Heracles has to bring King Eurystheus the girdle of the queen on which so much emphasis is laid in our picture. But more important for the painter than such associations is the actual encounter of the enemies: the army of women is seen here as so strong that only a Heracles could conquer it.

Pl. 5c   With her own weapon, the magic of her beauty, woman establishes her superiority over man. Thus Helen is the cause of mighty deeds, and in her abduction by Paris this truth finds a form which has continuously stirred the human heart. Perhaps we are justified in identifying as Helen the woman with abundantly flowing hair and a love-wreath who can be seen on a vessel in London. Her abductor, who clasps her around the wrist, is about to board a magnificent large ship with many oarsmen; but the figures of the couple, Paris and Helen themselves, are even larger than the actual ship. The painter was less interested in the episode itself than in the fateful significance of the scene.

Fig. 1   A pithos from Knossos shows another couple who have also been connected with an abduction by sea; the little pedestals on which the figures are standing were thought to represent the upper works of a ship, and the figures themselves were taken to be Theseus and Ariadne. A more characteristic theme from the Ariadne-legend, however, is Theseus' victory over the Minotaur, whereas the legend of Helen is usually illustrated by the abduction. No interpretations of this odd scene have, as yet, been established. It has even been explained as a wedding of gods but what, then, is the significance of the structures on which the two are standing?

In a search for further early illustrations of the Trojan War we practically fail to find representations of any of the incidents which we know from Homer's famous poems. There is none of the glorification of the heroes but, instead, only incidents of a profound seriousness in which there is already a suggestion of the spirit of tragedy.

Pls. 32a, b   There are a number of seventh-century paintings which show two scenes of a gloomy grandeur taken from the destiny of Ajax. Their expressiveness does, however, suggest that they may go back to creations of the later eighth century BC. If this is so they are the only early illustrations of the conflict at Troy which we possess.

After Achilles, the strongest of the Greeks at Troy was Ajax. The more hopeless the situation becomes the firmer his constancy grows. When Achilles was slain by Paris' arrow, Ajax was the only warrior who could rescue the Pl. 32b   dead Achilles, in his divine armour, from the battlefield. As a reward for this deed the weapons of Achilles should have been his due. But the wily Odysseus managed to induce the Greeks to accord the weapons to him. Athene laid a destructive madness on the eyes of the deeply offended Ajax. Raving, he slew cattle under the illusion that he Pl. 32a   was raging among the faithless Greeks. On awakening from his frenzy Ajax found his honour so greatly impaired that he threw himself on his sword. As in the lay of the Wrath of Achilles, the hero's greatness is apparent in his passionate behaviour. From these scenes it seems legitimate to suppose that Homer had also created a poem on the greatness and death of Ajax.

The nucleus of another poem of this type may have been formed by the evil excesses of the Greeks in their conquest of Troy. After having no success in their attempts to conquer Troy in battle, they are finally aided by a trick of Odysseus. The Greeks withdrew to the neighbouring island of Tenedos leaving before the city only a large wooden horse, ostensibly a dedicatory gift for Athene, the goddess of Troy. We have already encountered this horse on the Pl. 6a   delicately engraved Geometric fibula with the scene of Heracles and the Hydra; we meet it again on one of the most powerful of Early Archaic illustrations of legends. On the fibula engraving the wheels on the horse's feet are

26

2 Death of Astyanax. Fragment of an Attic Geometric vessel. Length 19 cm. (7¹/₂ in.). Post 750 BC.—Athens

3 Odysseus and Circe (?). Handle from fragmentary Late Geometric vessel. Height 8 cm. (3¹/₈ in.). Before 700 BC.—Ithaca

clearly recognizable, as is the high neck and proudly held head; but on its body we can discern rectangular trap-doors, the hatches through which the Greeks, hidden inside the horse, are to climb out. The clumsy stiffness of the construction indicates that it is made of wood; the long-necked birds all around the amazing work appear all the more animated. On the back of the fibula are five warriors advancing in step: these are the Greeks who, in well-ordered ranks, break into the city from outside (as in Fig. 39)—a feature of the story which we know from later literary versions.

The Trojans were credulous enough to drag the horse into the sanctuary of Athene, even breaching a section of the wall to do so, despite the warnings of the priest and priestess, Laocoön and Cassandra, to beware of the 'gift of the Danaans.' Inside the horse were hidden the doughtiest warriors. When the Trojans were asleep, weary after the celebration of their supposed victory, the Greeks climbed out of the horse, opened the city-gates, and admitted their comrades. A terrible massacre began. The Greeks' sacrilegious acts in their destruction of Troy brought the wrath of the gods down on their heads and, in punishment, many of them perished on their return home. One such evil act was the murder of little Astyanax, Hector's son. An Attic Geometric sherd is thought to show Achilles' son, Fig. 2 the barbarous Neoptolemus, holding the boy as he prepares to murder him; to the right stands the mother holding up her hands in despair. The Homeric age has selected some surprisingly sinister elements from the legend of Troy.

Of the many legends about the homecoming of the Greeks those concerning Agamemnon and Odysseus have particularly occupied artists. It may be that we already have a portrayal of Odysseus on a Late Geometric oinochoe: Pl. 8 on it we see a hero who is the only one of all his companions to save himself from a shipwreck by mounting the keel of the capsized ship. It is possible that this hero is Odysseus, soon to arrive on the island of the divine nymph Calypso. Whilst he is there Calypso lets him enjoy the life of a god; she would like to make him her immortal consort. But, although he stays for seven years, Odysseus never loses the homesickness which is the cause of his eventual return to the life of men. Unwilling as she is to release her lover, Calypso obeys the orders of the gods Fig. 45 and helps him to build a raft for the voyage home. Odysseus is carried to the land of the legendary Phaeacians who escort him home. In Ithaca Odysseus kills the suitors who are importuning the faithful Penelope. The scene on the oinochoe reminds us of these basic elements of the lay of Odysseus and brings to mind the patient sufferer of immense travail who, alone of all his companions, is finally to reach his destination.

But Odysseus was sitting weeping on the shore,
his spirit consumed with sighs and tears,
looking, as always, longing and disconsolate
over the barren sea.

But all day, every day, this remains my desire,
to journey home to my own land.
If a god must shatter me on the wine-dark sea,
I will endure it, patient, long-suffering.
I have met already many disasters
on the waves and from war: one more may be borne.

Odyssey V, 82–84, 219–24

A later poet extended Homer's *Odyssey*—or so it is thought—by making Odysseus relate, whilst he is staying among the Phaeacians, a large number of the adventures encountered during his journey, which are unnecessary to the poetical continuity of the original. The story of Circe, daughter of the Sun-god, had a particular influence on later art. Like Calypso, Circe lives on an island and, like Calypso again, she is in love with Odysseus. But the simplicity of this main motif is enriched by a subtle additional element: Circe is an enchantress who has already changed many shipwrecked sailors into animals, thus subjugating them to herself. This same fate befalls some of Odysseus' comrades. But he breaks the enchantment, having been warned by Hermes, and frees his companions. It has been supposed that the figure on the neck of a certain Late Geometric oinochoe represents some such enchantress. But, as is the case with many paintings of the Homeric period, the interpretation is uncertain.

One certain fact, however, is that at this time mythological scenes and figures were occurring side by side with the Geometric images which we have shown to be archetypal life-images. It would seem reasonable to understand the creation of mythological scenes as a response to the poetry of Homer. As in Homer's lay of the Wrath of Achilles, the greatness of the heroes is apparent in the passion of their inner emotions. This is how we must understand the victory of Zeus over Typhon, of Apollo over Heracles and of Heracles over Amazons and monsters; but it also explains the daemonic beauty of Helen, the greatness of Ajax and his injured feelings, the evil deeds of the conquerors of Troy and the lonely endurance of Odysseus. It has been inferred that the actual poems of Homer were short epics which would certainly correspond to these images. They bear witness to the existence of the connected series of tales which we have compared with the type of composition characteristic of the Geometric style.

At a later period, probably in sixth-century Athens, these epics were extended to form long epic poems in which the whole sequence of legend—from the creation of the world to the Doric migration—was given literary form. These poems are known as the Epic Cycle; we will see how their style is echoed in the visual art of the sixth century. The cyclic epics, which survive only in fragments and repetitions of the tales, therefore complete the work begun as early as the Geometric period by the great forerunners of Homer: the systematic and historical amalgamation of the legends. Fifth-century writers of tragedy select from the cyclic epics certain individual figures and interpret such heroes on the basis of the inner necessity of their being. The relationship between tragedy and the cyclic epics is thus similar to that between the Homeric epics and the earlier tales of the Geometric period. Homer also picks out individual figures, with a sure insight into the fundamental passions of mankind.

Fig. 3

Pls. 3a, b

Pls. 4a, b
Pls. 5–7
Pl. 8

I will remember   and not neglect
far-shooting Apollo;   the gods fear him,
tremble as he walks,   rise from their seats
as bending his bow   he passes through
the house of Zeus.   Leto alone
stays at her place   by thunder-loving Zeus.
She unstrings his bow,   closes his quiver,
takes them in her hands   and hangs them on a pillar,
on a golden peg   in his father's house.
Then she takes him   and places him in his throne.
The father gives him nectar   in a golden cup,
welcoming his son,   and the other gods
take their seats there,   and Leto rejoices:
she has borne a bow-bearing   and a mighty son.

Homeric Hymn to Apollo, 1–17

With the change from the Late Geometric to the Early Archaic style the narrative style also acquires a different character. We will first of all compare a painting showing Zeus and Typhon, produced *c.* 680 BC, with a Late Fig. 4, Pl. 4a Geometric representation of them. If the expressionistic art of the earlier period had corresponded to a new and noble view of the individual, the picture is now constructed and arranged on its surface with greater regularity.

4   Zeus and Typhon. Protocorinthian lekythos. Height 7.4 cm. (2¹⁵/₁₆ in.). Second quarter of seventh century BC.—Boston

The action is seen not merely as a fact or the assertion of the great individual, but as part of a connected whole, the inevitability and duration of which is expressed in the structure of the picture based, as it is, on firm axes and bounded surfaces. The lack of balance between different elements is not to be explained as a result of incompetence but, rather, as the result of the grand scale of the inner conception. The eagles around the tripod may indicate the power of Zeus, but the strange running figure of a sword-bearing daemon has still not been explained.

The style of the painting is reminiscent of that of the earliest hymn which has come down to us under the name of Homer, but which is most probably the work of a later, seventh-century poet. The hymn begins with a description Pl. 10 of Apollo's solemn entry into Olympus. On an amphora from Melos dating from *c*. 650 BC the same spirit pervades the portrayal of Apollo's arrival. The horses which form the teams of gods are frequently winged as they are shown here. The women standing in Apollo's chariot may be the Hyperborean virgins whose tombs were exhibited on Apollo's island of Delos. During the winter months Apollo lived among the Hyperboreans, a legendary people of the unknown northern regions of Hellas. Now he is returning home where he is welcomed by his sister Artemis.

5   Meeting of Apollo and Zeus accompanied by other gods and goddesses.
Bronze cuirass from Olympia. Height approx. 44 cm. (17$^{1}/_{2}$ in.). *c*. 650 BC.—Now lost

30

The scene has the character of a monumental painting. The hymn tells how the island of Delos burst into flower for joy at the birth of the god and, here too, plants of every kind surround the fabulous splendour of the divine procession.

An amphora from Naxos and a bronze cuirass from Olympia show two other, only slightly earlier processions of gods. On the amphora we see Ares and Aphrodite—in many places worshipped as a divine couple—standing in a chariot. The cuirass shows Apollo, again followed by two women (Muses or the Hyperborean virgins), going to meet a bearded god, presumably Zeus, who is accompanied by two younger, beardless gods. The artist's intention is not to depict the epic richness of legend but to portray great and dominating individual figures in their set relations to the environment. This art expresses the pride, felt in the Archaic period, in offering a firm basis of reality rather than mere fabulous stories. In a similar way, Antilochus, in a roughly contemporary poem, states a preference for the tough man of war of his time over Homer's aristocratic heroes.

Every period is characterized by its preferred themes. In the legends of the gods we can distinguish four such themes: the birth of the gods, their battles, their love-affairs and their assemblies. In the Early Archaic period, processions of the gods form the predominant theme, although others do occur—we have met the subject of strife among the gods in the Typhon-painting, and the ivory relief which shows the punishment of Prometheus suggests even darker associations. The Titan's son kneels, facing towards the right and leaning far back as he supports himself on his arms which are chained to the ground. His head is raised in agony and he appears to gaze out of the picture as the eagle, with widespread wings, swoops down from the right to tear at his liver.

Prometheus, whose name means 'forethought,' had originally created men from clay and stolen fire from Olympus for them. In later days people imagined how he had taught them skill and wisdom after Athene had breathed life into them. One mysterious ancient sacrificial custom was explained as originating in the teaching of Prometheus who taught men to cheat the gods by giving them only the skin and bones of the sacrifice and eating the flesh themselves. Meuli's explanation of this custom is given on p. 12. At any rate the concept of a Titanic opponent of the gods, who threatens the dominion of Zeus, is an ancient one (cf. p. 17).

Everything is subject to change, even the overlordship of the gods. Only the iron rule of Fate is imperishable, holding sway over everything, even over the gods themselves. This power could be alluded to by various names. One was Themis, goddess of Justice, morality and order. The son of Themis was Prometheus and to him she betrayed a terrible secret: should Zeus have a son by the sea-goddess Thetis this child would overthrow his dominion for, by the will of Fate, the son of Thetis is to be mightier than his father. Prometheus refuses to reveal this secret to Zeus who consequently chains him to a rock in the Caucasus Mountains where he lies in eternal torment. His distress is aggravated by the eagle of Zeus tearing at his liver which daily grows whole again to entice his tormenter. Eventually Heracles comes along and dares to kill the eagle with his arrows. Prometheus discloses the secret and is set free by Zeus. Zeus gives up all claim to Thetis and marries her to Peleus who fathers Achilles on her. Thus the will of Fate is fulfilled and this time Zeus' overlordship is not endangered.

Doric art, as Kunze has observed, does not know the intervention of Heracles and the rescue; in Attic art, on the other hand, we have many and varied illustrations of this episode from the late seventh century onward. This fine imaginative invention, by which the fate of Zeus is linked with the prophecy of Themis and the wisdom of Prometheus, may thus go back to Attic poetry of this period in which an attempt had already been made to make a cyclic whole of widely scattered legends dealing with everything from the creation of the world to the Trojan War.

From these later elaborations we return once more to a more straightforward type of narrative with the illustration of one of Zeus' love-affairs. A relief-decorated amphora from the island of Tenos shows him, transformed into a

Pl. 9

Fig. 5

bull, carrying Europa on his back through the sea. The legend tells how, one day, as the daughter of the Phoenician king Agenor was playing on the sea-shore with her friends, Zeus approached her fawningly in the shape of a bull and lay down at her feet. When the bold girl sat on his back he sprang up and carried her away over the sea to Crete where he made her the mother of the famous line of Minos.

Pl. 12 Although later artists could depict such events with greater richness, the birth of a god was never more nobly portrayed than on an amphora of the same style in Athens. Here the goddess is probably Leto who is depicted in a standing position as she gives birth to the divine children Apollo and Artemis; all around her we see assisting goddesses of childbirth, Eleithyiae. On either side there is a roaring lion similar to the marble lions of Delos; these are an unsophisticated, powerful expression of the poor island's marvel at the fact that such gods should be born there. Leto was a mistress of Zeus and jealous Hera forbade any country to give her rival sanctuary for the birth of her children. So Leto wandered about seeking shelter until, finally, the small rocky island of Delos dared to aid her. For this act the island was rewarded with the glorious sanctuary of Apollo.

Pl. 13 On a relief-decorated amphora of this style, recently found in the sanctuary of Demeter on Tenos, we have what is probably a representation of the birth of Athena from the head of Zeus. The solemnly enthroned, winged figure is characterized as male by the smoothly fitting, short chiton (cf. Perseus in Pl. 15b and Theseus in Pl. 27 a, b). Among the surrounding winged figures we can recognize, on the left of the picture, the goddess of childbirth Eleithyia who is wearing a girdled peplos and holding a sickle-shaped instrument in her right hand. On the right of the picture squats a young, naked god who is feeding the fire under the tripod; but the flying figure at the top appears to be there to receive the new-born goddess, recalling the Horae who greet Aphrodite as she emerges from the sea in, for instance, the famous relief on the Ludovisi Throne in Rome. All the divinities possess enormous eyes, a powerful chin and thick hair, yet all are quite different in their hairstyles and in every feature of figure and face. Note the smallest of the faces, that of Athene: her hair is the longest, falling over her cheeks and neck; she is depicted as screaming for her mouth is open, and the expression is intensified by the section of the helmet framing her face.

Pl. 15a Another scene which stands in this tradition of the mysterious and grandiose epiphany of a god is engraved on a mitra from Axos in Crete—a mitra was the stomach protection in a suit of armour. The delicately balanced composition of the engraving can only be understood as a late continuation of the Early Archaic style. Once again a pair of lions accompanies the manifestation of a god. This time the god is emerging from a tripod; we see his head, full-face, framed by long, flowing hair, whilst his body is covered by a shield with the emblem of a polyp; beside the figure we can see the hilt and end of a sword. Whether the presence of a tripod means that we can identify this god as Apollo is doubtful; there are, in any case, eagles perched on the handles of the tripod. Once again the contrast between the delicacy of the actual form of the god and the huge scale of the whole scene is peculiar, but the execution shows the subtle restraint of Cretan art. N. M. Kontoleon explains the tripod as the bath which is mentioned in the hymn to Apollo. After his bath the child Apollo partakes of the food of the gods and then assumes the shape of the fully-grown god. But the god on the mitra is most likely to be Zeus who was especially revered on Crete and was also worshipped in the form of an armed god.

> She flung her arms   around a palm tree,
> bowing her knees   to the soft meadow;
> the earth beneath smiled.   The god in her womb
> leapt to the light;   the goddesses shouted;

then, great Phoebus,   they washed you clean
with fresh water   and wrapped you in white,
in a new-made cloak   and a golden belt.
The mother did not feed   Apollo golden-sword,
but Themis poured nectar   and sweet ambrosia
with her divine hands.   Leto rejoiced:
she had born a bow-bearing   and a mighty son.
But when you had taken   the immortal food
the golden belt   no more had strength
to contain your body: you broke your swaddling-bands,
snapped the belt.   Then Phoebus Apollo
spoke these words   to the immortal goddesses.
'The lyre shall be mine   and the curved bow,
and I shall pronounce to mortals   the infallible will
of father Zeus.'   So he spoke,
Phoebus the far-shooter,   and began to walk
on the wide-pathed earth.

Homeric Hymn to Apollo, 117–34

It is tempting to suppose that the precious, Cretan-style ivory group, from which the figures of two women are preserved in New York, also illustrated a myth of the gods: the elder of the two women is looking majestically   Pl. 14 towards the left and has let her cloak drop; the younger figure, more slender and with delicate breasts, is fastening her girdle (not, as has been thought, loosening it). It brings to mind Aphrodite's magic girdle which endowed its wearer with all charms and which she lent to Hera so that the latter could appear irresistible to Zeus. In the *Iliad* XIV, 159 ff., Hera entices Zeus to unite with her in love on Mount Ida; this is to prevent his helping the Trojans as had been his intention. This story is one of the later parts of the *Iliad* but its roots are undoubtedly in earlier literature. It is obvious that these two noble-looking women were practising this type of love-enchantment, but, apart from this, we can give no interpretation of this representation of aphrodisiac power.

Then Aphrodite   took from her breasts
her embroidered girdle,   source of all her charms:
therein was love,   longing, and the careless
chat of lovers   that can beguile the wise.

She hastened to Gargarus,   high peak of Ida.
There Zeus saw her,   Zeus the cloud-gatherer,
saw, and was o'erwhelmed   by such desire
as when he first lay with her,   enjoying their love,
sleeping together   unseen by their parents.

Iliad XIV, 214–17, 292–96

In the Early Archaic and High Archaic periods the legends concerning Perseus and Bellerophon, of all the heroic
Pls. 15b ff. legends, were the most splendidly illustrated; this was because form could be given to the most individual daemonic experience by depicting the monsters they attacked. There must have existed a poem about Perseus in which the extraordinary daring and deeds of the hero were explained as a result of Athene's aid and which, for that very reason, gained rapid popularity in Athens. Perseus is the conqueror of the Gorgon Medusa, a spectre of such dreadful aspect that all who see her are turned to stone. Where Geometric art had chosen only to represent the divine cosmos, the pattern of the world, artists are now venturing to depict the incomprehensible which is a threat to all such order, to depict horror and death. But the fact that even Medusa is given a place in the divine order is profoundly Greek. Like her two sisters Medusa is a granddaughter of Uranus and Gaea; and she becomes the mistress of Poseidon. When Perseus cuts off her head two beings spring from her body: the winged horse Pegasus and Chrysaor of the golden sword. These are the offspring of her union with Poseidon. But the two sisters of Medusa, the Gorgons Stheno (the Strong) and Euryale (the Wide-wandering), who are as frightful in appearance as was Medusa herself, live on. Every victory, like that of Perseus, is no more than an episode in the never-ending battle of life.

Perseus was the son of Zeus and Danaë. Danaë's father Acrisius had been told by an oracle that he would be killed by his grandson. He therefore imprisoned Danaë in a brazen chamber, which was imagined to be like a Mycenaean tholos-tomb. But Zeus came to her there in the form of golden rain. When Danaë had given birth to Perseus, Acrisius exposed the two of them in an ark, which the sea carried to the island of Seriphos. There Danaë and Perseus were given protection by Polydectes, the king of the island. When Perseus had grown into a hero of great strength, Polydectes gave him the task of fetching the head of Medusa. Athene advised him to go, first of all, to the grey-haired Graeae, who were the sisters of the Gorgons and the embodiment of old age. They possessed only a single eye and tooth amongst the three of them. Perseus stole both as a pledge and refused to return the eye and tooth until the Graeae told him the way to the Gorgons. They also equipped him with a helmet of invisibility, a pair of winged sandals and a wallet in which to carry home the head.

Pl. 15b An early seventh-century relief-decorated amphora shows Perseus in the act of severing Medusa's head from her body. His face is turned aside because the sight of her would turn him to stone. Medusa has not yet been given the form of a girl with a Gorgon's head, as she is later portrayed, but is in the form of a Gorgon-headed mare;
Pl. 4a this recalls the hybrid creature, comprising horse and man, which we have already met in an illustration of the Typhon-legend and which expresses the Greek idea of dreadfulness. Delicate, tall, creeper-like trees—plants of the country of the gods—form a frame to the dreadful scene. The amphora was discovered in Boeotia but it belongs to a genre most abundantly represented on the island of Tenos.

Pl. 16 The painting almost a foot high on an Attic amphora in Eleusis, the most powerful representation of this legend, is a little later in date than the fine work from the Ionian islands described above. On the left of the scene Medusa is collapsing; her two sisters, Stheno and Euryale, their dreadful heads encircled by writhing serpents, follow in pursuit of Perseus. Their teeth are bared and they seem to glare out at us, a common device in Archaic art when the artist wished not merely to depict some extraordinary scene but to make it grippingly real. Athene, a tall, slender figure holding a spear in her right hand, is moving towards the terrible creatures to defend Perseus against them. The structure is more austere than that of the Ionian picture, although the contrasts between its elements are much more violent: for instance between the huge, glistening white legs of the Gorgons and their tiny arms which can never reach Perseus; or between their faces, looking like mixing-bowls, and the small delicate face of Athene on her very slender, white-clad body or the neatly agile, athletic legs of Perseus.

The pursuit of Perseus was also represented in the frieze of painted clay tablets in Aetolia, the only Greek monu- Pls. 18–21 mental cycle of paintings which has been partly preserved in original fragments. Whilst the entablature was still made of wood these square plaques of baked clay were placed, as 'metopes,' between the 'triglyphs' of Doric temples. The inscriptions and the style show that this metope-frieze is the product of a Corinthian workshop. It was produced at the very end of the Early Archaic period, in the phase of its final refinement. Many works of this phase, such as the Gorgon's head, at the same time anticipate the new colossal volume characteristic of the High Archaic Pl. 19 period.

The figures of the pursuing Gorgons in the Perseus-cycle are missing but, thanks to an old water-colour copy, Pl. 18 we are able to recognize the slim, rapidly moving figure of the victor from the attitude which, in Archaic art, depicts a running gait, *i.e.* very bent knees and arms held at a sharp angle. His feet and helmet overlap with the border of the picture so that the figure is freed from the architectonic frame and seems, in actual fact, to be flying before our eyes. By his bold rejection of restrictions, as well as by other means, the artist attains a new fullness of expression, even though, in acquiring finer proportions, he has sacrificed that noble element of fantasy characteristic of earlier art. The contrast between the delicate details and the bold form of the bared limbs produces a new kind of monumentality. It is only in looking at the original that one is able to feel the broad swing and elasticity of the curves, and the same applies to the delicate feathers on the winged sandals, the plaited border and the rosette on the girdled chiton and the eyes in the Gorgon's head, half hidden in the wallet under Perseus' right arm. Under the wallet we can discern a sword, fastened to a band laid diagonally across his chest. There is no filling ornament of the type we have so frequently seen on Archaic vases to indicate the surrounding landscape. In these metopes the figures are intended to give an effect of plasticity as in the actual relief-metopes which, at a later date, accompany the stone entablature of the temple. The framing band of rosettes takes the place of the filling ornament. These rosettes are one of the forms in which the life of the Greek building is embodied in a careful pattern and order; such forms become increasingly elaborate, culminating in figure-decorations and the actual cult-image. The whole is a 'cosmos,' a world completely under the sway of the gods.

This same order is also suggested in the colours which reduce the richness of a variegated scene to a few shades: black for the hair, the frame, the outline of male bodies, etc.; white for female flesh and for many details (Pl. I); red for the background to the rosettes, the outline of female bodies and other details; brown for male flesh and related Pls. 20, 21 yellowish and reddish shades for the general background. In paintings on marble the black is replaced by blue: blue and black were felt to have the same value. All the vividness of reality is thus suggested through the juxta-position of dark and light and through the use of red, the colour of blood and life, and of brown, the colour of the earth.

In case we should regard all this too lightly, however, it is fortunately possible to reconstruct one of the metopes in which the whole space is occupied by the head of a Gorgon. It might, indeed, be more accurate to describe it as Pl. 19 overrun by the head for, here once again, the interior motif overlaps the border: in the top right-hand corner we see the thickset, powerful head of a snake. There is a strong contrast between the elegance of the framing border and the glaring, squinting eyes and the huge mouth with its grinning teeth; but the repulsiveness is kept within limits by nobility of line and colour. Terror has been mastered and fitted into the cosmos.

At the time when the Thermos metopes were being produced another artist, possibly a Spartan, created the elegant ivory relief for the Sanctuary of Hera on Samos. This shows Perseus striding towards the right and gazing Pl. 17 out of the picture as he grasps one of Medusa's snaky locks with his left hand and severs her neck with the sword in his right. Although the Gorgon is already collapsing her fine plumage still swirls upward. The oblique position of the hideous face is oddly effective; shown in any other way we should scarcely be able to bear it beside the handsome figure of the conqueror. There are other elements to support our belief that this is an illustration of the triumph of Perseus: the helmet of invisibility, again overlapping the border, and the figure of Athene to the left of the bold warrior, speaking eagerly to him and touching him benevolently with her hand. The relief is Spartan in type, but the delicate modelling of rounded forms, especially the heads of Athene and Medusa, has an East Greek quality which the artist has incorporated into his own style.

Pl. 44b   The subsequent adventures of Perseus are not represented artistically until a later period. As he was flying home he saw Andromeda chained to a rock. Her parents were forced to sacrifice the princess to a sea-monster because her mother had insulted the Nereids by claiming that she was more beautiful than they. With the help of the Gorgon head Perseus slew the monster and set Andromeda free. The children of the couple included Perses, the ancestor of the Persians. Later Perseus accidentally killed his grandfather Acrisius with a discus-throw.

Pl. 20   The frieze of painted clay metopes in Thermos includes three other surviving illustrations of legends. In the one which is justifiably the most celebrated we see two women, Chelidon and Aëdon (the swallow and the nightingale), mourning a dead child. The legend has many versions but it is unlikely that Thermos would have known it in the Attic version which is the most familiar one, concerning the Thracian king Tereus who had married the Attic princess Procne. As she felt lonely in the remote northern regions Procne asked Tereus to fetch her sister Philomela. The barbarian did as she asked but, on the journey home, violated Philomela and cut out her tongue so that she could not betray him. But the clever Philomela had the idea of embroidering her story into a robe and thus communicating it to Procne. In revenge Procne killed her son Itys and gave his flesh to the father to eat. When the horrified Tereus learned of the monstrous deed he pursued the sisters but was turned into a hoopoe which constantly cries 'Itys'; Procne became the nightingale Aëdon which constantly laments and sings; and Philomela became the swallow which can only twitter. It was Roman poets who first, by a confusion of names, made Philomela the nightingale.

The most clearly recognizable figure in the surviving part of the metope is that of Chelidon who is standing on the right with the remains of the finely patterned robe below her. Particularly well preserved is her head in which, as is common in ancient portraits, the face predominates. The eye has an unforgettable penetration and the ear is the most delicately delineated in all Archaic art. There is, as yet, no sense of the volume of the head, because the facial expression predominates over everything; but the hair, shoulders and arms display a roundedness which lends the bowed upper body an urgent intensity. The contrast between the angle of both bodies and the frame of the picture strengthens the emotional effect of the former. The figure of Aëdon, which has suffered more damage, was originally the more prominent due to its somewhat larger build and its more bowed position; she would have been so portrayed as the mother of Itys whose dead face can be seen above Chelidon's lower arm.

Pl. 21   The mighty hunter portrayed in one of the metopes may be Orion about whom there were many legends, but only one is told: the handsome giant, who could walk on the sea, was a lover of Eos, goddess of the Dawn. He wooed the daughter of Dionysus' son Oenopion, but the latter made him drunk and put out his eyes—for what reason we do not know. The blinded Orion sat a boy on his shoulders to act as a guide and was led by him eastwards across the sea. When he was touched by the first ray of the sun he regained his sight. For a long time he was a hunter in the retinue of Artemis but she finally killed him for some act of sacrilege. This legend is one of the very ancient ones which were in many ways obscure even to the Greeks of historical times.

36

The hunter carries a boar and a hart on a pole laid across his left shoulder—only a hero would be capable of carrying such a tremendous load. The elasticity of his step is wonderfully contrasted to the rigidity of the frame. The foremost leg is bearing rather more of his weight, and the front of the pole, where the booty is hanging somewhat lower, is slightly inclined: these features all serve to intensify the forward thrust of the movement. Much of the fine and variegated pattern on the chiton and, more important still, the bearded head with the thick long hair

6   The daughters of Proetus (?). Clay metope from Thermos. Height approx. 88 cm. (34¹/₂ in.). *c.* 625 BC.—Athens

Pl. 18 of a man of the open air are better preserved than the corresponding parts of the very similar figure of Perseus and therefore help us to gain a clearer idea of the appearance of the latter.

Fig. 6   The fifth of the metopes shows two girls uncovering the upper part of their bodies. Dörig thinks they are the daughters of King Proetus of Tiryns. On visiting the sanctuary of Hera they had boasted that their father's palace was more richly furnished. As punishment Hera inflicted them with madness. They went raging shamelessly through the forests, and it was only by sacrificing twenty young heifers to Artemis that their pious father could prevail on the goddess to intercede with Hera and so restore the maidens to their senses.

In Homer, Bellerophon, the hero of Corinth, is not, like Perseus, Heracles and Theseus, the son of a god. He was originally an oriental hero who was given a place in Greek legend when Corinth became an important city in the Geometric period. His grandfather was Sisyphus, the most cunning of all men and a son of Hermes. From Athene, Bellerophon received the gift of the bridle, that simple and yet infinitely effective means by which men were enabled to tame the horse. With Athene's aid Bellerophon himself was able to master the wonderful horse Pegasus; she also helped him actually to find the winged horse as he grazed beside a spring. Since Pindar, Bellerophon is also known as a son of Poseidon.

Whilst Bellerophon was staying as a guest of Proetus in Tiryns, Stheneboea, the wife of the king, fell in love with him. When he rejected her advances, she made false accusations against him to King Proetus. The jealous husband gave Bellerophon a letter of introduction and sent him to Iobates, King of Lycia. In actual fact the letter Pl. 22   contained a request to get rid of Bellerophon. So Iobates sent him to fight the Chimaera, a fire-breathing creature with the foreparts of a lion, the hind-parts of a dragon and the body of a goat. However the hero succeeded in slaying the monster and, after coming safely through many other dangers, won the hand of Iobates' daughter together with half his kingdom. In the end the possession of Pegasus proved his undoing. In attempting to fly up to Heaven he was thrown to the ground and lamed, after which accident he passed a lonely old age. Where Pegasus had pawed the ground the last time Corinth's miraculous fountain, the Spring of Peirene, spurted up; and thereafter Pegasus fed at the manger of Zeus.

The early illustration of Bellerophon's battle with the Chimaera clearly shows the Corinthian master's pride in the young hero whom he portrays as shouting as he hurls his spear. The curves of the monster's outline are delineated with an indescribable delicacy and tenseness; the artist has held his imagination in check to a greater degree than Pl. 16   his Attic contemporaries whose style we know from the Eleusinian amphora. There is already an anticipation of the subtler proportions found in the Thermos metopes but, whereas these show Archaic art in its noonday maturity, the Bellerophon scyphus still appears as a clear summer morning.

Of all the deeds of Heracles which we met in the Homeric period, Early Archaic artists picked out, in particular, the fights against Centaurs. This was because those hybrid creatures, comprising horse and man, were felt to be especially dreadful, as we saw in connection with the legends of Typhon and Perseus. But there was also apparently another, deeper reason. The most important of Heracles' fights with Centaurs was the one with Nessus, the signi-Pl. 6c   ficance of which we discovered on a Late Geometric gem. The outcome of Heracles' passionate love and hatred was to be his death on the pyre and, ultimately, his translation to Olympus (cf. p. 24).

Pl. 24b   In one Spartan ivory relief we are made to feel more for the fate of the strange, powerful Centaur Nessus than for Heracles himself. Having overtaken Nessus the victor now grasps him by the hair and thrusts his sword through his body. The supple giant's helpless gesture and fainting look as he collapses are contrasted to the powerful figure of Heracles, his head framed by curls and his eyes looking decisively out of the picture. The lack of balance in the

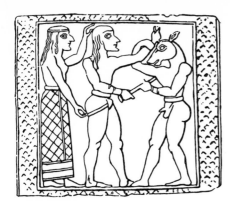

7 Theseus slaying the Minotaur. Gold relief. Width 4 cm. (1¹/₂ in.). *c.* 650 BC.—Berlin-Charlottenburg

scene, especially apparent in the smallness of the victor's torso, shows that the work is rather more archaic than the early Bellerophon illustration.

Pl. 22

We do not know which version of Nessus' deception of Deianeira was in the mind of the painter of the New York amphora. In one account Nessus gives her some of his seed as a charm. At all events the painter has thought of the future doom and has therefore included the figure of Deianeira, portraying her seated in the chariot. We can see her robe to the left of the chariot-wheel and the reins in her right hand. The figure of Heracles is still shown in the style of monumental painting, *i.e.* not Black-figure; he has grasped Nessus by the hair and is drawing his sword. Nessus has collapsed and stretches his hands out imploringly. The agitated owl above Nessus may indicate Athene's aid. It is astonishing what a wealth of colour and what powerfully stern and rugged nobility the painter has wrung out of his technique. The pair of fighting animals on the neck of the vase intensifies still more the savage quality of the scene.

Pl. 23

Now we can also understand why the High Archaic painter of the Melian amphora laid such stress on the parting of Heracles and Deianeira. Any Greek looking at the scene would think of the doom consequent on Heracles' love: his third illicit love-affair is to be the immediate cause of his death. We have a representation of this tale, dating from the High Archaic period, on the Corinthian krater in the Louvre. This shows a rich banquet in the palace of King Eurytus of Oechalia on Euboea. As is the custom, the Princess Iole goes up to Heracles to offer him greetings. The guest has stopped eating and, raising himself up, looks at the beautiful girl who begins to feel uneasy under his gaze. She wraps her cloak closely around her—how expressive the one visible finger is—and looks around anxiously at her father. Iole's family refuse to give her to Heracles who then savagely murders the king and his sons, burns the palace down and carries off Iole as booty. Deianeira, grown jealous, gives Heracles a garment which has been smeared with Nessus' charm and which, when he puts it on, corrodes Heracles' flesh. The unhappy man builds himself a funeral-pyre on Mount Oeta and finally, through death by fire, enters Olympus.

Pl. 57c

Pls. 60a, III

Another Centaur, Pholus by name, entertains Heracles as his guest. They open a wine-jar during their meal but the scent of the wine attracts other Centaurs whose behaviour grows so insolent that Heracles is forced to drive them away, thereby killing many. One of the wounded Centaurs brings Cheiron an arrow which has been dipped in the Hydra's poison; in scratching himself with the arrow Cheiron receives an incurable wound. To rid himself of his torment he renounces his immortality in favour of Prometheus. From the picture it is obvious that the painter is particularly fond of the vivid figures of the hairy, supple Centaurs, although he also shows affection for the kneeling archer who, alone, makes himself master of all this wildness of nature.

Pl. 24a

The story of Theseus and his deeds, as told in the Attic epics of the late sixth century composed under the influence of the noble family of the Alcmaeonidae, was so closely assimilated in that of his friend Heracles that it is difficult to discover its original parts. The nucleus of the legend is formed by the rule of Theseus in Mycenaean Athens, which he is supposed to have actually made into one city by giving all the scattered communities of Attica a common acropolis. Another original element is his victory over the Minotaur which is repeatedly illustrated; even in early

Pl. 7 representations Ariadne is portrayed as his helper. Ariadne was the daughter of the King Minos of Crete who had imposed on Athens a tribute of seven youths and seven maidens to be sent yearly as a sacrifice to the Minotaur. The bull-headed giant lived in the Labyrinth, a palace in which anyone, even if he were not a victim of the Minotaur, would wander hopelessly lost and finally perish: an ancient symbol of the other world. Theseus had volunteered to be one of the seven youths. In Crete he won Ariadne's love, as we are shown in a few scenes of violent courtship

Pls. 27a, b and shy response. Ariadne gave him a ball of thread by which means he could find his way back out of the Labyrinth after overcoming the Minotaur.

On the neck of a man-high, relief-decorated amphora in Basle, the earliest illustration of the fight with the

Pl. 25a Minotaur, we see, in the lower frieze, Theseus and Ariadne throwing stones at the Minotaur whilst, above them, two pairs of the Athenian children help in the task. The Minotaur is still given the form of a river-god with the body of a bull and a horned, human head, not, as later, the form of a bull-headed man. At the Minotaur's feet we can see the ball of thread and, leading from it, the actual thread to which they must all cling if they wish to find the way back out of the Labyrinth. The stature and position of the fighters in the front rank make them only slightly more prominent. The artist is not depicting daemonic passion as in the Homeric Age, but rather the dignity and the significance of the episode, as in the processions of the gods and the Hymn to Apollo.

Pl. 13 The vigorous distinction between partners, which we came across in the Birth of Athene on an earlier vessel of this type, is now refined and restrained. There is a great contrast between the elegant horses and the powerful bull. Another surprising feature is the difference from the more free and forceful expression of Attic works; the huge, relief-decorated amphora has a different intrinsic monumentality recalling the clear light and sharp winds of the islands.

Pls. 50, 51 Theseus fled with Ariadne and the liberated youths and maidens sailing first of all to Delos, where the famous victory-dance was performed, and thence to Naxos. There, according to one beautiful account, which may only date from Late Archaic times, Theseus was visited during the night by Athene who took him away from Ariadne's side because they were both destined for different lives. 'Ariadne' was originally only an epithet for the great Mother Goddess. Now Dionysus, the divine lord of the rich island of Naxos, comes to Ariadne to make her his consort.

Theseus, however, returns to Athens. Of all the deeds of the ruler of Athens, the people of antiquity were especially proud of his part in the battle of the Lapiths and Centaurs. The leader of the Lapiths, Zeus' son Perithous, was a friend of Theseus and had invited both him and the Centaurs to his wedding. The lascivious Centaurs tried to rape

Fig. 8 the women and a savage fight ensued. We may already have an illustration of this wedding on a gold plaque of *c.* 700 BC. A bronze plaque of the end of the Early Archaic period shows, for the first time, the death of the Lapith,

Pl. 27c Caeneus, an episode which, at a later time, was frequently illustrated in modified versions. Caeneus had originally been a girl whom Poseidon had ravished. When Poseidon promised to fulfill anything she might desire she asked to be changed into a man so that she need never again suffer such violence. At the same time Caeneus was made invulnerable. The Centaurs were therefore unable to overcome him in any other way but by driving him into the

40

8 Wedding of the Lapiths (?). Gold relief, thought to be from Attica. Length 22 cm. (8⁵/₈ in.). *c.* 700 BC.—Berlin-Charlottenburg

ground like a stake. The bronze relief shows him fighting with two swords—the very image of defiance. Caeneus was also notorious for his irreverence. It was not, however, the intention of the artist of this relief to depict the dramatic qualities of the episode. He is concerned with the person and the dignity of the antagonists. There is only a slight suggestion that the head of the Centaur on the left, towards whom Caeneus is turned, is raised higher, that he is reaching up to grasp the plume on his enemy's helmet and that the knotted roots of the tree-trunk, which he wields as a weapon, is extended further away from him. The picture has a lyric, ballad-like quality of depth and immediacy, so that even the forest, the home of the wild Centaurs, is suggested with a particular affection.

Let us look back at the illustration of the legends of Bellerophon, Perseus, Heracles and Theseus. In the artistic representation of such heroes, the Greeks have learned to regard the individual in a different way, to see him not as accidentally individual, not merely as the product of great passion, but in the unity of his character and fate. Bellero- Pl. 22 phon, the hero with the winged horse, is distinct from Perseus with his winged sandals. The flight of Bellerophon contains a premonition of his downfall, the temptation of one whom the gods have raised too high. Perseus is a different type of hero; he is the pious conqueror of the Gorgon, winning the head of Medusa for Athene's aegis. Pls. 15b, 16–18 Heracles and Theseus, unlike Perseus and Bellerophon, are not winged. Heracles is not merely the passionate lover, Pls. 23, 24a, b but is also the mighty fighter who triumphs over the savagery of nature. Theseus is the clever and intelligent young Pls. 25a, 27a, b man who wins Ariadne's love. Common to all these four very different heroes is the fact that they all fight fabulous creatures, as distinct from the joint enterprises of the Argonauts, the Seven against Thebes, the Calydonian Hunt and the Trojan War.

Let us now note which episodes in these joint enterprises were thought daemonic enough to be represented with the same seriousness and given the same significance as the fights with the Chimaera, Medusa and the Centaurs. Surprisingly enough what we find are the fates of Helen, Achilles, Ajax, Agamemnon and Odysseus, whereas the Calydonian Hunt, the Voyage of the Argonauts and the Theban legends are still unrepresented.

Theseus is even connected with events taking place before the Trojan War. When still very young, Helen was abducted by Theseus and Perithous, who took her to their city of Aphidnae in Attica. But the Dioscuri brought their sister home again untouched. A Protocorinthian lekythos shows the divine brothers, the Dioscuri, on the left; Fig. 9 they can be identified by the fact that they are mounted. Helen has turned towards her rescuers and has raised her arms in the gesture which signifies the miraculous manifestation of a god. The painter has also given prominence to the figure of Helen by making it so much larger than the others. Theseus, holding a spear in his left hand, clutches at Helen's left wrist whilst, behind him, Perithous comes to his aid, brandishing a sword. On another lekythos the Fig. 10 abductors are not represented. It shows only the mounted Dioscuri and, between them, a goddess with shield and spear. A small female figure is taking refuge with the goddess and holds on to her sword-arm with one hand. These

41

9 Helen, being taken home by the Dioscuri. Protocorinthian lekythos. Height 7.1 cm. (2¹³/₁₆ in.). *c.* 680 BC.—Paris

Pl. 26 two lekythoi help us to interpret the main scene on the extremely finely engraved metal cuirass recently discovered in Olympia by N. Yalouris. It shows Helen wearing a high crown as on the lekythos in Fig. 10 but, as in Fig. 9, she is standing between two pairs of young men and is turned towards the pair on the left. We may therefore assume that this pair represents the Dioscuri although, in this case, they are not mounted; the portrayal of the whole episode is gentler and more restrained. The artist is more concerned with the representation of matchless beauty and the distinctions between the personalities than with the dramatic aspects of the episode. He was undoubtedly a Cretan

Pls. 27a, b like the other artists of early illustrations of abductions which we have met.

Pl. 29b We return to Corinth with the celebrated Chigi vase on which, for the first time, we have a representation of the Judgment of Paris. It appears as a small, restricted scene, side by side with many magnificent friezes showing chariot-races, battles and hunts. Unfortunately all that remains of Hermes, who leads the procession of goddesses, is the tip of his herald's staff, and of Hera, Athene and Aphrodite, we have little more than the heads. We nevertheless feel the thrill of the miracle of divine glory appearing on earth—a bewitching and fateful centre in all the wealth of surrounding life.

The parents and the childhood of Achilles, the male counterpart to Helen, provide other themes. The scene in

Pl. 28 which a young hero wrestles with a daemonic woman, whose eyes look straight ahead, is more likely to depict

Pl. IV Peleus' conquest of Thetis than the wrestling-match between Peleus and Atalanta after the Calydonian Hunt, for the

10 The Dioscuri and Helen (?). Protocorinthian lekythos. Height 6.5 cm. (2⁹/₁₆ in.). Early seventh century BC.—Oxford

last-mentioned group of legends was not well known until the High Archaic period. Atalanta, in any case, would be a partner of equal stature to Peleus and not a goddess of mysterious superiority.

The wrestling-match between Peleus and Thetis is probably also shown on a fine Cretan plate. The figure of Figs. 11, 12 the hero is sketched in outline; he has long hair and a pointed beard, is wearing sandals and carrying a finely ornamented sword at his belt. With both hands he clasps a gigantic fish as it rears up to the left—this is the shape into which Thetis has changed herself. But the size of the plate is great enough to allow the whole figure of Thetis to be shown further to the left: the white-painted foot at the bottom must be hers. Buschor's reconstruction shows her fleeing to the left, running with the knees conventionally bent.

The offspring of the union between Peleus and Thetis is Achilles, who is to cause his mother so much pride and so much sorrow (pp. 85–92). Peleus hands him over to the Centaur Cheiron to be educated. A hoard of Early Attic vases, dedicated in a sanctuary on the island of Aegina, contained fragments of an amphora which illustrated this scene. We can discern the Centaur and the arm of Peleus holding the child Achilles, in a forest of magical ornament. Pl. 29a The boy is wearing a cloak of distinction and the face of Peleus is embellished by a flower over the forehead. When he is older, the boy receives from his mother the precious armour forged by the god Hephaestus. On the neck of Pl. 24c an amphora from Delos we see the light, slender figure of the hero as he faces Thetis and, between the two, a helmet and shield with the emblem of a lion. The earlier illustrations of the presentation of the armour do not correspond to the story as we know it from the *Iliad*, *i. e.* how Thetis brings Achilles new divine armour after the death of Patroclus. This episode belongs only to the later phase of the *Iliad*. In earlier literature the younger hero was already equipped with divine armour.

The Aegina hoard is also the source of the monumental pedestal to a mixing-bowl; it shows Menelaus, who is Fig. 13 designated by an inscription, leading the Greek princes assembled for the Trojan campaign. The proud bearing and magnificent costumes of the men correspond to the magnitude of the event; no later epoch has been so successful in depicting the significant essence of an event on which artists of this period concentrated; they were not interested

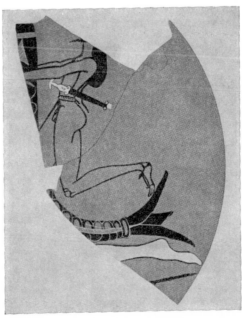

11, 12   Peleus wrestling with Thetis (?). Plate from Praesus, sherd and
reconstruction. Diameter approx. 35 cm. (14 in.). *c.* 650 BC.—Heraclion

13 Menelaus assembling the Greek princes. Early Attic pedestal. Height of surviving fragment 68 cm. (26³/₄ in.). Before 650 BC.—Berlin

in relating all the manifold details of an episode. The heroes are therefore not further differentiated; only Menelaus is given more empty space about him and is holding his head at a slightly higher angle than the rest. The swifter rhythm in the frieze of horses intensifies, by contrast, the dignity of the princely procession.

Artists are silent on the subject of all the troubles of the Greeks in their preparations for the campaign. Similarly they give no representations of the sacrifice of Iphigenia, daughter of Agamemnon. When the Greeks had eventually reached Troy and all attempts to take the city, by sudden attack or by negotiation, had been frustrated, it soon became difficult to feed the army. The most common of the expedients to which they then had to turn was a plundering expedition. The actual opening of the Iliad is apparently preceded by some such expedition in which Agamemnon has claimed Chryseis, and Achilles Briseis, as booty. Among all pastoral peoples cattle-rustling was considered an act of knighthood. Thus we hear how, on Mount Ida, Achilles steals the cattle of Aeneas, the doughtiest hero of the Trojans next to Hector. In the fight Aeneas flees, Achilles kills the cattle-herds—amongst them a son of Priam—and Pl. 25b drives away the cattle. A relief-decorated amphora in Boston shows Achilles kneeling in front of the line of stolen cattle as he lies in wait for the armed men who intend to retrieve them. We can see the spears in his hands, the shield at his side and, above, the towering plume of his helmet.

Another ambush by Achilles, carried out at the beginning of the campaign, may be illustrated on an unguent-bottle from Corinth, painted c. 650 BC: the assault on Troilus, youngest son of King Priam. The episode will be

44

described in detail when we come to the epic phase (below, p. 87). A similar, though slightly later vase, which is a jewel of draughtsmanship, shows Patroclus setting out to battle—an anticipation of the richer departure scenes that we find in the epic phase (Pl. 29c). That it should be precisely the name of Patroclus which is inscribed beside the warrior indicates his relevance to the story of Achilles and his wrath.

From the *Iliad* itself only a single Early Archaic scene—but a very significant one—has been preserved. It is on an amphora of the Tenos type and shows Hecabe, Queen of Troy, walking in procession with her maidservants to Pls. 30, 31 bring a precious robe to Athene, the city-goddess. The splendour and dignity of the procession is reminiscent of the Attic painting showing the departure of the heroes. Such dignity befits the important figure of the queen, the mother of so many proud sons, who is finally to live through the death of them all and the fall of her house and to become the slave of the son of Achilles. Hecabe is holding the sceptre; she is taller and more dignified than the four maidservants carrying the robe. The impressed patterns on the garments shine out like stars.

> But she went down   to the scented storeroom
> where she kept her robes,   the colourful work
> of Sidonian women . . .
>
> Hecabe took
> one of these   as an offering for Athene,
> the stateliest robe,   most richly embroidered:
> it shone like a star   from beneath the others.
> She hastened away,   many ladies with her.
> But when they reached   the temple of Athene
> on the acropolis,   the doors were opened
> by fair-cheeked Theano . . .
>
> She took the robe
> and placed it on the knees   of Pallas Athene.
>
> *Iliad* VI, 288–89, 293–98, 302–3

Artists were occupied less with the *Iliad* than with the deaths of the heroes Achilles and Ajax. After the fall of Hector, the shield of Troy, it seemed that the city was lost. But help came to the Trojans in the persons of the Amazons, under their Queen, Penthesilea, and Memnon, King of the Ethiopians; the Amazons came from the north and the Ethiopians from the east, so that the outermost limits of the known world were drawn into the events. The legend of Penthesilea is not represented artistically until the High Archaic period, but Memnon's duel with Achilles already adorns the neck-painting of the tall amphora from Melos. Memnon's father, Tithonus, was a brother   Pl. 10 of Priam, and his mother was Eos, goddess of the Dawn. Thus both heroes are the sons of divine mothers: Achilles of Thetis and Memnon of Eos. Thetis and Eos, full of anxious forebodings regarding the fate of their sons, intercede in the duel. Achilles, the victor, must be the warrior on the left as this is the usual position for the victor. The fact that the woman on the right—presumably Memnon's mother—is not wearing the veil which designates the married woman would agree with this interpretation. The goddess of the Dawn is the perpetual unhappy lover. She loves

14   Paris slaying Achilles. Protocorinthian lekythos from Perachora.
Height 10.3 cm. (4¹/₁₆ in.). *c.* 680–670 BC.—Athens

both Cephalus and Orion without requital and is even forced to lament her husband Tithonus because, in asking the gods to grant him eternal life, she forgot to ask also for eternal youth. So eventually he shrivelled up into a cicada which could do nothing but chirp.

Fig. 14 Shortly after the conquest of the Amazons and the Ethiopians, Achilles is killed by the arrow of Paris, guided by Apollo to Achilles' heel because the son of Thetis was destined to die young. We have already heard how Ajax rescues Achilles' body, how he is nevertheless cheated out of the armour of Achilles and how he throws himself Pls. 32a, b on his sword. The frequency of these scenes suggests that they occupied artists of the day more than the actual sack of Troy.

The most affecting picture of the atrocities committed by the Greeks in their conquest of the city came to light only recently on a vase of the already familiar type of the relief-decorated amphora. It was discovered on Mykonos, Pls. 34, 35a the neighbouring island to Tenos. The neck is dominated by the Wooden Horse. Its wheels and trap-doors, as well as the erect position of the horse's neck, show that it is the same type as its forerunner on the Late Geometric fibula. But here the surfaces are sketched in with lines of a taut intensity which can be seen at their most delicate in the slender legs of the Horse. The structure of the relief as a whole is lucid and powerful, with decisive gradations in size-relationships. In the openings in the side of the horse the heads of the boldest warriors are visible; but we can also see their arms on which they are carrying splendid weapons with which they will arm themselves as soon as they are set free from the restricted space of the Horse's body: a helmet, a shield and two swords in their scabbards are recognizable.

The five heroes advancing from the left could be taken to be the Greeks breaking into the city, as shown in other representations of the conquest. The emergence of the Greeks from the Horse may therefore be linked to an event which is chronologically later; thus the two warriors moving to the left, one of whom is brandishing a spear in his right hand, are to be interpreted as Trojans opposing the Greek invaders of the city. The Trojan on the bottom right has set one foot on the Horse's wheel so that it looks as though the two are fighting with the men concealed inside the Horse. Yet by all accounts, the heroes in the Horse met no resistance when they emerged.

Even more remarkable are the scenes in the friezes around the shoulder and belly of the vase; they are richer than on any other vase of the type. We might expect the well-known scenes of the conquest of Troy to be the most prominent: the murders of Priam and Astyanax, the father and son of Hector, the threatening of Cassandra by Ajax Pl. 35b and of Helen by Menelaus. It is true that a few of these scenes appear to be intended and it may be that the very

46

picture which is missing, from the centre of the shoulder, contained just some such scene. But much more to the fore is a veritable Massacre of the Innocents, with Greeks, in every sort of situation, threatening and murdering Trojan boys in the presence of their desperate mothers. This particular crime of the Greeks must have been felt to be especially serious. They are to pay for it, as for the other evil acts committed in the conquest of Troy, with all the suffering and destruction which overshadowed their homecoming. This mood contrasts strongly with the passionate heroic concepts which we met in the Homeric Age, in particular on the shield of Tiryns. The age of Archilocus, Pl. 7b *i.e.* the age of the early lyric, opposed the epic tradition with keen criticism and a new sense of reality.

> Not for me the general renowned nor the well-groomed dandy,
> Nor he who is proud of his curls or is shaven in part;
> But give me a man that is small and whose legs are bandy,
> Provided he's firm on his feet and is valiant in heart.
>
> ARCHILOCUS, *Fragment* 55 (Translated by A. Watson Bain,
> from *The Oxford Book of Greek Verse in translation*,
> ed. T.F. Higham and C.M. Bowra. Clarendon Press, 1938)

An Early Archaic fragment of a bronze relief can be linked with a scene which, from the High Archaic period onward, is frequently illustrated: Menelaus at last faces the unfaithful Helen. It is the intent of the deeply injured husband to kill her, but Aphrodite has given Helen such beauty that the weapons sink uselessly in his hands; and this very couple is the only one to enjoy years of peace after a swift and safe journey home.

The fate of Agamemnon is all the more terrible. By ill-fortune he receives, along with much other booty, Priam's daughter Cassandra, the unhappy prophetess who, after rejecting Apollo's love, had suffered the punishment that nobody ever believed her prophecies. Agamemnon's consort Clytaemnestra bore him a bitter grudge because, at the departure of the Greeks for Troy, he had sacrificed his own daughter Iphigenia to placate Artemis. In Agamemnon's absence Clytaemnestra had committed adultery with Aegisthus. After welcoming her returned husband with feigned tenderness she murdered first Cassandra, of whom she was jealous, and then Agamemnon himself. In the Argive bronze relief from the Sanctuary of Hera the figure of Cassandra—slender and with splendid, flowing hair—has Pl. 32c a nobility which contrasts it to the coarser figure of the murderess. The clay relief from Gortyna portrays Clytaem- Pl. 33 nestra even more dramatically. Agamemnon is seated in the centre on a magnificent throne, his body shown in profile towards the left; in his left hand is a spear, his sword is slung and his eyes look out of the picture. Aegisthus, who has come up on him treacherously from behind, grasps the upper end of the spear in his left hand whilst, in his right hand, he holds some object over Agamemnon's head. This object is presumably the fatal net which the coward has cast over the head of the King. Clytaemnestra, coming from the left, holds the net with her left hand whilst, with the dagger in her right, she stabs the great king.

But it was a period deeply stirred by the idea of revenge. Clytaemnestra had sent Orestes, her son by Agamemnon, to be reared in the home of an old friend. On reaching manhood, Orestes, with his friend Pylades, came home in disguise intending to avenge his father. One of the Early Attic vases from Aegina shows Orestes, like a black Pl. 36a avenging spirit, as he grasps Aegisthus by the knot of his hair and threatens him with his sword; Clytaemnestra flees to the right clutching her cheeks in horror. In another version of the episode, on a bronze mitra from Crete, we see Orestes threatening an enthroned Clytaemnestra; here, in Orestes' matricide, we are made aware of the full terror of the revenge and all that is dreadful in the unnatural crime which is the source of all his further suffering. (The mitra has not yet been reproduced.)

The figure of Aegisthus is given greater importance on the shield-strips of the High Archaic period, which show him enthroned. By analogy with these, Kunze believes that the same scene is shown on the Ionian relief-decorated amphora in Boston: the usurper sits enthroned in the centre, turned towards the left. Orestes rushes at him, clasping with his left hand the arm which Aegisthus has stretched out in entreaty, and lunging with the sword in his right. Behind Aegisthus, Clytaemnestra, a spindle in her right hand, holds up her arms in horror. This Ionian relief and the Argive-Corinthian shield-strips give Aegisthus and Clytaemnestra greater dignity than they are accorded on the Attic vase where the story is told more dramatically. The dignified conception may stand closer to the literary model whose existence we may infer from all these Oresteia scenes. In this literary version Clytaemnestra must have been the main character, standing as a dark antitype to her bright sister Helen. It may well be that one of the short epics which we inferred for the Homeric Age was devoted to the figure of Clytaemnestra. Many of these epics, like that of the Wrath of Achilles, could actually stem from Homer himself.

Pl. 32c   The bronze relief showing the death of Cassandra surpasses all these other pictures in the nobility of the conception and in the powerful language of its finely nuanced narrative. The scene at the top of this bronze plaque shows a warrior, his sword in its scabbard, pursuing and laying hold of a woman who is carrying a spindle; the bold swing of her robe suggests that she may be turning towards her capturer. This is not a representation of an abduction, as characterized by the legend of Paris and Helen; it is an assault on a struggling woman. The figures could possibly represent Theseus and Helen (cf. Fig. 9, Pl. 26).

Odysseus' recital, at the Phaeacian court, of his earlier adventures must have formed part of the original *Odyssey*, one of the Homeric poems. In the later *Odyssey* this tale was extended to a narrative comprising three books. The centre of the narration is the description of the adventure with the Cyclops Polyphemus, for Odysseus' revenge on Polyphemus, who was a son of Poseidon, brought the wrath of the gods upon him, thus giving rise to the disasters

15   Blinding of Polyphemus. Sherd from a krater. Second quarter of seventh century BC.—Argos

48

I Blinding of Polyphemus. Amphora from Eleusis. Height 1.42 m. (56 in.). Painting on neck. *c.* 670 BC.—Eleusis. Cf. Fig. 15

of his subsequent adventures. Such was the importance of this episode that the blinding of Polyphemus is illustrated in three paintings from the Early Archaic period and, at a later date too, the incident is represented with extraordinary frequency. The fabulous tale, with its island setting, recalls the story of the nymph Calypso even in the description of the landscape.

The barbarous, one-eyed Polyphemus is one of a race of giants whose ill-breeding is dramatically and grimly contrasted with the manners of men. Instead of receiving Odysseus and his companions hospitably, as he should, he imprisons them in his cave and rolls a great boulder, which only he with his giant's strength can remove, before the entrance. Then he devours two of the companions for supper and four more the next day. For Odysseus simply to murder Polyphemus as he slept would have been useless, for who would then have removed the boulder? But Odysseus, with his cunning and patience, is not at a loss: he makes Polyphemus drunk and then boldly drills through the giant's eye as he lies in a deep sleep, using for the purpose a huge stake, the end of which has been previously hardened in the fire and which he can only lift with the help of his friends. The blinded giant awakes with a roar, finding himself no longer able to catch the Greeks. In the morning he lets his flock out into the open, examining the sheep with his fingers as they go. But between each pair of sheep Odysseus has tied a man, whilst he himself clings Pl. 37 to the belly of a great ram. The finest of the Attic vases from Aegina shows the heroes escaping in this manner. The painter finds particular pleasure in nuances of colour. The whiteness of the bodies stands out from the clay background and the shimmering fleece of the rams with which it was quite customary to compare the bloom of masculine youth. The middle ram, possibly the one on which Odysseus himself hangs, is baring its teeth and holding its tensed head rather higher than is the ram behind which carries one of the companions holding fast, with both arms, to its horn.

If we compare these two Cyclops-paintings we find that the Argive one tells the story more realistically, as it were, showing the straw on which Polyphemus is lying and also a greater disparity between attackers and attacked. The Attic painting retains more of the passionate grandeur of Late Geometric art, combining this with the strict pattern Pl. 16 and order which we have already met in the Perseus-painting on the same amphora.

THE HIGH ARCHAIC PERIOD

The Colossal Style

In the decades *c.* 600 BC the Archaic style reaches a mature perfection. We have already met examples of the style in the amphora with the departure of Heracles and in the krater with the banquet of Eurytus. Where painters of the Pls. 57c, 60a, III Early Archaic period had produced a solid structure within the surface, artists are now introducing the third dimension: the rounded contours of their forms take full account of the curved surface of the vase. Instead of a decorative and superficial arrangement of elements, we have an articulation of bodies which opened the way to the development of the Colossal Style in the sculpture of the time. The contrast between relatively small linking elements and the uninterrupted main forms brings about the monumental effect of timeless, divine existence. The style was founded by the Dipylon Master in Athens and its effect quickly spread to other regions, as may be shown by the group of Cleobis and Biton, a work of the master Polymedes of Argos dating from the beginning of the sixth century BC. Pl. 38 In this work the new fullness is already combined with a warm portrayal of the characters, but it is significant that the work depicts no actual episode.

The story of Cleobis and Biton does not, strictly speaking, belong to heroic legend, for the two brothers are not members of one of the heroic families of the 'Age of Bronze'; we do not know when they lived. Other men of the 'Age of Iron' were also revered as heroes and exalted in songs and statues: they include great poets, generals and champions, the 'seven wise men' and many philosophers, but in particular the tyrant-killers Harmodius and Aristogeiton. They stand somewhere between legend and history, as will become clear from a look at the two Argive brothers. One day the team of bulls, which their mother, the priestess of Hera, was to drive from Argos across the hot plain to the temple, had failed to arrive; so the brothers harnessed themselves to the chariot. On arriving, exhausted, they fell asleep and the priestess prayed that her sons should be granted the best possible fate. In answer to this prayer the goddess let their sleep be an eternal one and, after this, they were honoured like the heroes of legend; heroic statues of them were dedicated in the Temple of Apollo at Delphi. This mythological outlook thus isolates certain figures of lasting quality and places them outside the fleeting course of history.

> Stars around the fair Selene
> hide away their radiant faces
> when she is full and shines her brightest
> over the earth ...
>
> SAPPHO

The Early Archaic period had had something of a hymn-like, lyrical quality. Now, in the age of Sappho, lyrical language becomes richer and more mature. Amongst all the images of gods, one of the surviving Greek wooden

Pl. 39 reliefs is particularly impressive; it shows the holy wedding of Zeus and Hera. The interpretation is made certain by the eagle of Zeus over both figures. The wedding of Hera was celebrated annually in each of her temples. By bathing in the river she repeatedly recovered her virginity and was married anew to Zeus. Connected with this is the famous episode in the *Iliad* which was discussed on p. 33. Hera approaches Zeus who finds her so irresistible that he at once sinks with her to the earth which sends up soft grass and all kinds of flowers to be their marriage-couch. The wooden relief still retains something of the Early Archaic, two-dimensional quality. The earlier period had already produced many representations of divine couples: Zeus and Hera themselves on Spartan ivory reliefs;

Pls. 9, 10 Ares and Aphrodite, Apollo and Artemis on Ionian amphorae. But the new image has a warmer and more intimate, yet at the same time more powerful effect in the new apprehension of existence.

An Attic oinochoe, painted *c.* 600 BC, as well as other vases and clay reliefs, shows a great winged figure whom

Pl. 40a S. Karusu has identified as Aristaeus, the great Nature-god of antiquity, who is the patron of the hunt, of agriculture and cattle-breeding and who sends the mild, fructifying winds. He brings precious gifts to men: the hoe and, in sealed bottles, oil, milk and honey, 'the tenth part of immortality'! The flanking lions intensify the magnificence of his appearance, as do Archaic animal-friezes in general when they celebrate such great lords of Nature.

Pls. 4a, 11a Of divine conflict we have already met two examples in the fight between Zeus and Typhon and the punishment
Pl. 41a of Prometheus. A bronze relief, produced at the beginning of the sixth century BC, shows the eagle flying, with spread wings, towards the chained prisoner. The Early Archaic relief had shocked us by its portrayal of physical agony. The confrontation, here, of the naked, defenceless giant and his tormenter is even more sinister in its effect. But we are soon to meet an Attic High Archaic representation in which we see Heracles setting Prometheus free.

16   Reconstruction of the gable from the Temple of Artemis on Corfu. *c.* 590 BC.—After H. Schleif

Fig. 16   The mightiest of divine battles can be seen in the gable of the Temple of Artemis in Corfu; and yet even this is subordinated to the monstrous figures in the centre of the gable: the running Gorgon is accompanied by her children Pegasus and Chrysaor. The legend tells how the children sprang from her neck when Perseus had cut off her head. Yet in the gable she is still uninjured and Perseus is not represented. The master of the gable was not concerned with telling the story of Perseus and Medusa but with giving a more precise definition of the monstrous being. She is not simply a grotesque mask, such as the people of antiquity used to hang on the ridge-beam to ward off evil; she is the mistress of Poseidon by whom she becomes the mother of Pegasus and Chrysaor. Thus even the most dreadful of beings proves to be a member of a divine lineage and order. Zeus' brother Poseidon has other fearsome descendants, such as the Cyclops who involved Odysseus and his companions in such peril. These relationships give expression to the terror and destructiveness characteristic of the ocean. Medusa herself and her sisters are the children of the sea-monsters Phorcys and Ceto, and the latter are the offspring of the good Ocean-god Pontus and Mother Earth.

52

17 Zeus fighting with Typhon. Shield-relief. Width of strip 7.2 cm. (2¹³/₁₆ in.). *c.* 580 BC.—Olympia

The powers of terror are, thus, not at the opposite pole to beings of light as in oriental mythology, but all are conceived as descended from the same mother. The bold arc and clearly defined forms of the gable, together with the regularity of the lay-out and the clarity and proportion of its parts, all accord with this conception.

The gable as a whole bears witness to the world and power of Artemis, in whose person the great Mistress of Life was worshipped in Corfu. In the right-hand corner of the gable, Zeus, the father of Artemis and king of the   Pl. 43 gods, hurls his thunderbolt at a giant who lifts his right hand in entreaty and covers his unprotected body with his left hand. The legend of the young hero who, by his cleverness, overcomes the apparently insuperable powers of a giant is told in many versions and among many different peoples. Our sympathy is as much for the victor as for the fate to which even the mightiest must succumb.

One opponent of Zeus whom we have already met is Typhon but, since he was conceived as a hybrid being, he   Pl. 4a cannot be the figure in the Corfu gable. However, like the giant in the gable, Typhon is at times characterized by a combination of gigantic size and helplessness; we must therefore be concerned, here, with figures which have some   Fig. 17 relation to Typhon. This characteristic is, on the other hand, never found in the Gigantes, a savage, heavily-armed race sent by Mother Earth, shining in brazen armour and with long spears in their hands, to do battle against the gods. We find no certain representations of the Gigantes until the Late Archaic period, when they are shown as armour-clad men fighting against all the Olympians. The legend of the Gigantes, as we know it, cannot therefore be represented in the Corfu gable, although this has repeatedly been asserted. We should have to assume that there was an earlier, lost version of the legend of the Gigantes, and, in so doing, stray far from the literary tradition.

The only remaining opponents of Zeus are the Titans, the older generation of the gods who, like the Olympians, form a family (p. 17). They were the children of the Sky-god Uranus and Mother Earth, Gaea. Fearing for his absolute sovereignty, Uranus tried to prevent the Titans from ever seeing the light. Mother Earth was aggrieved by this and so made a sharp-toothed sickle which she gave to her son Cronus. He lay in wait for his father, castrated him and threw the genitals behind him. Mother Earth caught the drops of blood and, from them, gave birth to the avenging spirits, the Erinyes, and then to the Gigantes and the ash-nymphs who, themselves, became mothers of another savage race. The genitals of Uranus fell into the sea and out of the foam arose Aphrodite, goddess of Love.

The liberated Titans married amongst themselves and Cronus engendered some of the Olympian gods. But, like his father Uranus, he would not let his children see the light because he wanted to retain his sovereignty over the world. So, to the grief of their mother, Rhea, he swallowed each of the new-born children. However, when Rhea had given birth to Zeus, she hid him and gave Cronus a stone, which she had wound in swaddling clothes, to swallow in place of the child. As soon as Zeus had reached manhood he overcame Cronus and forced him to give up the other children. He also liberated the Cyclopes who gave him the thunder and lightning, symbols of his power. The war between the Olympians and the Titans, who were finally banished to the Underworld, is supposed to have lasted ten years.

The Titans are thus beings of quite a different order from the Gigantes; they are not an armed race of the earth but an illustrious and sovereign family of gods. The rule of the Titans is overthrown by the Olympians, but, being immortal gods, they cannot be destroyed like the Gigantes, but only banished. The Gigantes attack the Olympian gods, but the Titans are forced to defend themselves against the Olympians. Men imagined an 'Age of Gold' under the rule of Cronus and, even in their banishment, the Titans were thought to dwell in a happy country of the gods. All these characteristics of the Titans fit the figure in the Corfu gable. Zeus' opponent is not an armed hero of the type of the Gigantes, but a giant; he is not a hybrid creature like Typhon, but has a noble human form. There is something venerable about him and he arouses our sympathy. Evidence for the enormous eyes as a characteristic of the Titans is abundant. The youthful and beardless form of Zeus also fits in with this legend, for the Olympians were, after all, a later generation of gods than the Titans. The contrast between the younger and older gods is re-echoed in literature (Aeschylus, *Prometheus*, 148ff.).

A final fact which supports the interpretation of this scene as the battle with the Titans is that Eumelus of Corinth formulated the legend of the Titans in an epic poem. His works are unfortunately lost but the accounts of them are important for Corfu because Eumelus was writing not long before the Temple of Artemis was built. It has already been conjectured that he had a direct influence on Corfu, which was a Corinthian colony. His Titan-poem was as striking and original as the image of the Titan in the Corfu gable. If we wonder how an artist of this period would represent the Titans we could scarcely imagine a better image than the one in the right-hand corner of the gable.

Pl. 42   The interpretation of the group in the left-hand corner of the gable is more difficult. An enthroned and augustly robed figure, in front of a wall of artistic design, is threatened by a great spear. It used to be supposed that the enthroned figure was Priam at the Sack of Troy, taking refuge from the barbarous Neoptolemus on the altar of Zeus. This interpretation might seem to find support in the fact that, elsewhere too, scenes of divine battles are coupled with scenes of Troy, although they are then always on two sides of the building and not in the same gable. The
Fig. 16 identification of the seated figure with Priam is made less plausible by the dead, naked giant lying behind him, who cannot easily be regarded as a Trojan. He can better be understood as a Titan similar to the Titanic opponent of Zeus, although his hair is rather more carefully arranged. We must assume that a similar fallen giant lay in the right-hand corner of the gable. For this reason there have been repeated attempts to explain the left-hand group also as a battle of gods.

Pl. 42   J. Dörig, with great industry and care, has explained the enthroned figure as Rhea, the venerable consort of Cronus, but such an explanation is questionable since, having once saved her children from Cronus, it is unlikely that Rhea would be attacked by one of them. M. Rabinovitch has conjectured—in conversation—that the enthroned figure, whose sex cannot be ascertained, could be the King of the Titans, the august Cronus, whilst the opponent of Zeus
Pl. 43 might be Iapetus or Atlas, both of whom are front-rank fighters in the war between Titans and Olympians. The fine wall behind the throne would fit in with this conjecture if interpreted as indicating the famous city of Cronus; similarly, the tree on the right, behind the group with Zeus, could stand for the divine garden of the Titans. Thus Dörig, with his ingenious identification of the battle-ground, could still be correct. Cronus' antagonist would then have to be Zeus' brother Poseidon. The discrepancy between these corner-groups might explain the contradictory

54

II   Medusa with Pegasus. Clay metope. Height 56 cm. (22 in.). *c.* 620–610 BC.—Syracuse accounts of the Titans in which they are sometimes described as lordly beings, like the enthroned figure, and some-times as beings with looks full of power and gloom, like the opponent of Zeus. Objections to the identification of these figures with Titans cannot be made on grounds of the immortality of the Titans: it is an ancient motif of divine combats that one of the partners must fall in a state resembling death and can yet live on. Castor, one of the twin sons of Zeus, also falls in battle but is nonetheless immortal. It is, in fact, part of the logic of battles that some warriors must fall. The logic of this view outweighs the logicality of the contents of the narrative. Despite all this the only certain interpretation is that of the corner-group on the right which we can accept as Zeus and one of the Titans; Corfu is one place where we must reckon with unfamiliar versions of the legend.

Artists of the High Archaic period considered it more important to capture and give shape to beings striking

Pl. II   terror—as in the central portion of the Corfu gable—than to tell a story. In Syracuse, a city whose art shows many links with that of Corfu, there is a rather earlier metope-relief dating from the beginning of the High Archaic period and, in this, Medusa is again holding Pegasus; the piece would thus appear to spring from the very same attitude of mind as the Corfu example. Other Syracusan works are also linked with this tradition. The Chimaera, Beller-ophon's antagonist (p. 38), is quite frequently represented alone or paired with another such monster; while we sometimes have to look for Bellerophon on the opposite side of the vase. Yet, in some Attic vases, a desire to tell a story nevertheless breaks through and this is to determine the style of the later High Archaic period. Some fragments

Pl. 40b   from the Ceramicus, which have been interpreted by D. Ohly, show the Chimaera standing with her back towards the hero as he springs at her. The underparts of her body have been completely transformed into a massive, bearded snake which, together with the uncommonly large fire-breathing goat, wards off the hero; the lion's head merely looks round menacingly.

In the Colossal style, however, an atmosphere of serenity prevails. Thus, in the main work of the Nessus painter,

Pl. 59   the great amphora in Athens, the Gorgons are represented alone without Athene and Perseus. In place of the rich
Pl. 16   narrative of the Eleusis amphora we now find the artist maturely restricting himself to the dark figures flying over the waves of the sea—a frieze of dolphins. On a rather earlier bowl, from the Aegina hoard, the painter has included
Pl. 44a   Perseus and Athene. The bowl originally had two metope-pictures on each side but, in some cases, only one of these has survived. The pursuing Gorgons are lost, but the figures of Athene and the fleeing Perseus have been preserved. Athene is not yet clad in armour as painters of the next generation portray her, but is wearing only a peplos and cloak; the inscription, however, tells us that here is the protectress of heroes. Of the paintings on the other side
Pl. 64a   of the vase only two flying Harpies have survived, their pursuers, the sons of Boreas, are missing. This two-dimen-sional-looking narrative painting, with its multiplicity of figures, is clearly more archaic than the painting on the Nessus amphora; nevertheless, when it is compared with the Eleusis amphora, it is obvious that the High Archaic style is emerging.

The graceful and lively frieze of an Attic dinos in Paris, which has the same theme, is, on the other hand, later

Pl. 45   than the Nessus amphora. A comparison of all these Perseus-paintings shows the development towards the Colossal concentration of form which we find at the mature stage of the High Archaic style, and towards a new organization and variety in narrative during the late phase. The four-horse chariots on the Paris dinos are not part of the Perseus-scene but belong to a battle-group on the reverse of the vase. Some of the horses nevertheless snort excitedly and toss their heads as if they were facing the barbaric Perseus-scene. Hermes, the Messenger of the gods, in a short, girdled chiton and with the great herald's staff in his left hand, comes warily from the left; he is wearing winged shoes and a sun-hat, held in place by a band. The goddess Athene shows greater confidence and self-reliance than

56

Hermes, as she walks before him, dignified in the long peplos and cloak and wearing a taenia in her hair. She is identifiable because, in narrative art, Hermes and Athene—who is the helper of heroes—are regularly shown as companions of the heroes. The beheaded Medusa, her wings still spread, is collapsing—more gradually and gracefully than in earlier art. The blood streaming from her neck is arranged in regular tongues like the snakes on the gigantic masks of the sisters as they rush ahead. Like Hermes, the Gorgons and Perseus are all wearing winged shoes and short chitons, but the chitons of the Gorgons are decorated with finer borders and the bodies of the winged women are more dainty than that of the powerful Perseus. His strides are longer than those of the Gorgons and his hair streams behind him in the wind; the movement of the whole scene increases from left to right. The chase speeds across the quiet body of the vase like a fleeting vision.

Flying towards his homeland Perseus caught sight of Andromeda, daughter of King Cepheus, chained to a sea-cliff. Cepheus' wife had boasted that she was more beautiful than the Nereids. As punishment for this Poseidon had sent a sea-monster to whom Andromeda had to be sacrificed. Perseus conquers the monster, sets Andromeda free and wins her for his wife. On a Corinthian belly amphora in Berlin, we see Perseus hurling stones at the monster, Pl. 44b whose boar-like head is all that is shown of it. The unusualness of the form is matched by the uncommon use of white paint. A red tongue lolls from the voraciously gaping jaws. Undulating water is suggested below the head. Perseus has a heap of stones near him and Andromeda is holding more in both hands. Her long, girdled chiton adds to the motley character of the painting.

This scene stands so far outside the tradition of vase-painting that it must have been stimulated by some other form of illustrative art. The popular dramatic quality in the narrative suggests one of the picture-books which could also have provided the models for other vase-paintings (cf. pp. 74, 96). The form of the panel amphora first appeared in Athens at the beginning of the Late Archaic period, c. 560 BC, and this shows that the Andromeda amphora must have been produced somewhat later, i. e. that it is one of the late continuations of the epic High Archaic style.

Besides the illustrations of the legends of the gods, of Bellerophon and of Perseus, which we have been discussing, the Colossal High Archaic style also produced some powerful scenes from the Heracles-legend as well as a represen- Pls. 57b, 59, 60a tation of the Harpies and some isolated Trojan scenes. Most of the representations of scenes from the cycles of Heracles, the Argonauts and Troy do not, however, appear until a later phase of the High Archaic style—a phase which brought to maturity the cyclic continuity of the narrative. The isolated scenes from our phase will therefore be discussed in the following section in which we will find a quite surprising change in narrative style.

In the Colossal style the actual story-telling element retreated further into the background than in the Early Archaic style. To compensate for this, reality was depicted with greater richness, roundedness and power, and Pl. 39 so were the relationships between the protagonists; we might think of Zeus and Hera, of Zeus and the Titan or Prometheus and the eagle. All accompanying motifs were suppressed, because the artist was completely engrossed Pls. 43, 41a by his dominant figures. This is the age of the poets Alcaeus and Sappho, whereas the Early Archaic period had been the age of the Hymn to Apollo and of Archilocus. The inscriptions on the dedicatory gifts bear witness to the artists' pride in the realism of their creations—a realism which no later age could achieve in such unbroken strength.

The narrative styles of poetry and visual art have never been so close as in the later High Archaic period in the first third of the sixth century BC. We have already met one example of this new type of narrative illustration, with Pl. 45 its multiplicity of figures, in the Gorgon dinos; but our most magnificent example is the krater by the painter Pls. 46–52 Clitias which is known as the François vase—a prince among vases. It may have been originally destined for the Acropolis where Attic painters used to dedicate the most splendid of their works. If so, it must have been traded to Etruria only because, in the firing, it turned out slightly reddish underneath instead of completely black. It is 60 cm. (2 ft.) high and is decorated with two hundred figures, excluding animals. Here the narrative is no longer merely balladic, as hitherto, but is truly epic; separate episodes are not simply picked out in isolation, but are bound together by intellectually conceived connections. At the same time we find all the traits which P. Von der Mühll thinks characterize the later poets who brought the *Iliad* and *Odyssey* to their present volume and compass: out of the poem about the wrath of Achilles evolves an epic of the Trojan War and out of the poem about Odysseus' homesickness a full account of all his adventures; the poem about the events leading to the deaths of Achilles and Ajax evolves into the *Aethiopis*, and the poem about Clytaemnestra into the epic of the *Nostoi*—the return of all the heroes, and so on. The poets of these cyclic epics brought the ancient short epics into broad, connected sequences. The *Titanomachia* dealt with the creation of the world and the conflict between the gods, the *Thebais* with the Theban legends, the *Cypria* with the history preceding the *Iliad* (judgment of Paris, abduction of Helen, youth of Achilles, etc.), the *Aethiopis* with the stories of Penthesilea, Memnon and the death of Achilles, the *Little Iliad* with subsequent events up to the Sack of Troy, and the *Nostoi* with the return of the heroes.

There is abundant evidence that Solon and Pesistratus collected the Homeric poems together. At the great festival of the goddess Athene the epics had to be recited as a continuous whole. There was evidently a desire to avoid fragmentation by isolating stirring, individual recitations. A need for greater profundity in parts of the poems was later satisfied by the creation of tragedy, which acquired its classic form *c.* 500 BC, but which must certainly have passed through preliminary stages. The closeness of the connections between 'cyclic epic' and tragedy is clear, for the latter is consistently dependent on the cyclic tales for its subject-matter. Whatever significance the new version of the epics had for the performance at the great festival of Athene—the Panathenaea—was consequent on the Attic forms of their language. Their popularity is attested by the large number of vase-paintings with cyclic themes.

The dating of this new version of the epics to the early sixth century is confirmed not only by the connection with contemporary literature, especially with Solon, but also by archaeology. Those very themes which P. Von der Mühll believes to have been introduced into the *Iliad* by later poets are now illustrated for the first time: these Pls. VI, 76b, a, Fig. 36 include the funeral-games for Patroclus, Priam's petitioning of Achilles, the renown of Diomedes and the story of Dolon. In addition there are stylistic connections which also find expression in the composition. Great legend-complexes are given unity by questions of guilt and atonement and, in the cyclic poems, also by oracles and other omens. Marvellous and superhuman elements are emphasized, because they are no longer taken for granted; everywhere there is mention of gods and miraculous signs, the gods themselves fight and quarrel and must be present everywhere. Another novel feature is seen in the frequent and surprising changes in the scene of events. In addition, a growing interest in historical facts has been observed in the *Cypria*.

An example of one of the links formed by guilt and atonement is already found in the first lines of the *Odyssey*—lines which are ascribed to the later poet. (How different are the first lines of the *Iliad*. Cf. above, p. 18.)

Sing to me, Muse,   of that resourceful man
who wandered far   after laying waste
sacred Troy.   He saw the cities
of many men,   and learned their manners,
striving to survive   on the high seas,
enduring great hardship   to lead home his companions;
but he failed to save them   in spite of his efforts,
for they were destroyed   by their wicked deeds,
fools, for they killed   and ate the cattle
of Hyperion's son,   Helios the sun-god:
he took from them   their day of return.

Odyssey I, 1–9

Emphasis on marvellous and superhuman elements in the work of the later poet:

Then Athene raised   high in the roof
her death-dealing Aegis: their senses deserted them.
They fled through the palace   in panic like cattle
distraught and stung   by the darting gadfly
in a long spring day.

Odyssey XXII, 297–301

Then brazen Ares   bellowed loud:
as great was the noise   as when nine thousand—
ten thousand soldiers   shout in battle,
fighting together   with the god of War;
trembling overcame   both Greeks and Trojans,
fear of Ares   insatiable in war.
As a black darkness   descends from the sky
when after burning heat   a blustering wind rises,
so to Diomedes,   son of Tydeus,
appeared brazen Ares   rising to heaven
concealed by clouds.

Iliad V, 859–67

The description of Athene's armour recalls her statue which is first traceable in Athens at the time of Solon.

She put on the cloak   of Zeus the cloud-gatherer,
and girded on her armour   for grief-bearing war;
she flung over her shoulders   her fearsome Aegis,

with Panic set round it   placed like a crown;
therein was Strife,   therein Valour,
chilling Attack   and the terrifying head
of the malignant Gorgon,   monster of Zeus.
She set on her head   her two-horned helmet,
with four gold bosses,   adorned with figures
of the fighting men   of a thousand cities.

Iliad V, 736–44

On the two sides of his krater, which is now in Florence, Clitias opposes the Attic hero Theseus and the pan-Greek hero Achilles. He has, however, much more to say about Achilles. His field of vision is wide, reaching back to the Hunt of the Calydonian boar, because Peleus, the father of Achilles, was one of the participants. We will see that this legend, which hitherto we had not met, is illustrated with particular frequency in this period, often together with the funeral-games for Peleus from the legend of the Argonauts and with scenes from the expedition of the Seven against Thebes. A Corinthian epic belonging to the period *c.* 600 BC is presumably the source. It has long been supposed that the description of the funeral-games for Patroclus was composed after the pattern of the games for Pelias. On the neck of the François vase, below the Calydonian Hunt, we actually have a representation of the funeral-games for Patroclus. Thus a cyclic combination, which was new at that time, has been adapted to fit the intentions of the painter.

When the fearsome boar was laying waste the fields of Calydon, heroes from every corner of the inhabited world came together to kill it. On the François vase one of the huntsmen bears the name of the Cimmerians who had become well known to the Greeks through their campaigns in Asia Minor *c.* 700 BC. The main heroes were Meleager and Atalanta; Atalanta was the first to succeed in wounding the boar, which she did with an arrow. Many of the huntsmen, among them Peleus, the father of Achilles, later followed Jason on the voyage of the Argo to Colchis to win the Golden Fleece. Meleager himself had died before this. According to a decree of the Fates he would live only until a certain firebrand was burned to ashes. His mother Althaea put the brand carefully away. But when Meleager had accorded the victor's prize of the boar's pelt to Atalanta and had killed his mother's brothers because they had opposed him, Althaea, in anger, threw the brand into the fire and Meleager had to die.

On the frieze of the Hunt, which runs around the neck of the krater, the foremost of the four pairs of hunters charging the boar from the left is formed by Peleus and Meleager; as the father of Achilles, Peleus had to be given prominence on Achilles' side of the vase. Atalanta and Melanion—who is later to win her love—form the second pair. Atalanta had been exposed as a baby, but she had been suckled by a bear. Later she was reared by some hunters and Meleager, who loved her, persuaded her to join the Calydonian Hunt. After Meleager's death she seems to have taken part in the expedition of the Argonauts, for her wrestling-match with Peleus was a famous episode, taking place after the expedition had ended, at the funeral-games for Pelias (to be discussed later). She finally decided to marry but let it be made known that she only wanted, as husband, a man who could overtake her in a foot-race. Anyone failing to fulfil the conditions would be killed. Melanion, however, was helped by Aphrodite. She gave him some golden apples which he let fall during the race. Atalanta bent to pick up the apples and so lost the contest. Now she herself was gripped by the power of Aphrodite. Seized by passionate love, Melanion and Atalanta embraced within the sanctuary of the Mother of the gods and were punished by being changed into the lions which draw the chariot of the great Mother. But we are also told of a son of Atalanta, Parthenopaeus, who later took part in the battle of the Seven against Thebes (pp. 81–82).

In the paintings, only one huntsman is killed by the boar: this is Ancaeus who had expressed the strongest objec- Pl. 47b
tions to the participation of a woman in the hunt. The first couple behind the boar consists of Castor and Polydeuces, the twin sons of Zeus; we shall meet them in the expedition of the Argonauts, of which they are most distinguished members, together with the next pair, Acastus and Admetus, the famous husband of Alcestis. The painting does not, on the other hand, show certain other heroes who, according to the legend, took part both in the hunt and in the voyage of the Argonauts; these include, notably, Jason, the leader of the Argonauts, and Amphiaraus who is to be the noblest figure in the later expedition of the Seven against Thebes.

Since Admetus does not appear in any other of our illustrations we should briefly tell the story of his strange fate. After the expedition of the Argonauts he won for himself Alcestis, one of the noblest of women. She would only marry a man who could yoke a lion and a boar together to a chariot. Apollo helped Admetus to accomplish this apparently impossible task. Later the god even acted as servant to the illustrious couple because Zeus had demanded that, to atone for a murder, Apollo should serve a mortal for one year. The house enjoyed marvellous blessings. When Admetus later fell ill, Apollo promised his recovery on the condition that somebody else died for him. Nobody, not even Admetus' life-weary parents, would consent to do this until Alcestis took upon herself this hardest of partings. But the valiant woman was brought back from Hades by Heracles.

The main frieze is worthy of its great theme since it runs for nearly five feet around the krater. In it we see all the gods coming to the wedding of Peleus and Thetis. Clitias may have been inspired by the pomp of the procession Pl. 48a
in the great festival of Athene, with which we are familiar from the Parthenon Frieze. Thetis sits inside her palace whilst Peleus stands before it at the altar, ready to receive the exalted visitors with an offering. Cheiron, the future teacher of Achilles, strides on ahead with the prey caught for the feast. Hestia brings the hearth-fire, Demeter the bread, Dionysus the wine whilst the Muses surround the chariot of the father of the heavens. Where Early Archaic processions had portrayed the dignity of individual gods, we are now faced with an image of all Olympus—an image which could only spring from the philosophical and organizing mind of the Greeks. The foundations are here laid for that differentiation of characteristic distinctions in the gods which we admire in the Parthenon Frieze. Other friezes on the François vase carry such differentiation even further than in the main frieze in which the exactly parallel poses of the pairs of gods riding in the chariots depict, first and foremost, the communal dignity and splendour of the Olympians.

The first scene, taken from the life of Achilles himself, belongs to the very beginning of the Trojan War. Achilles lay in wait for Troilus, the youngest son of King Priam, when he came to fetch water from the well-house with Pls. 48a, b
his sister Polyxena. Achilles now pursues him with mighty strides; he is going to kill him despite the fact that Hector and Aeneas are coming to Troilus' aid through the city-gates on the right. In the powerful legs of Achilles we can sense all his swift-footedness; the splendid hair of Troilus streams out behind him in the wind. Polyxena flees before him to the venerable Trojans, Antenor and Priam, who are surprised by the attack as they sit outside the gates. The Pl. 48c
three phases of Achilles' assault on Troilus—the ambush, the pursuit and the death of Troilus—are illustrated with exceptional frequency in the first half of the sixth century BC; the reason was that it was then thought that this wrong committed by Achilles was the cause of Apollo's anger. Even one of the gable-reliefs on the Acropolis of Athens is concerned with this theme. Troilus had taken refuge in the temple where Achilles killed him; as punishment Apollo later guides the arrow of Paris to the heel of Achilles. This explains why, on the left, we see Apollo following

18   Arrival on Delos of the children of Athens. Ariadne, her nurse and Theseus at the head of the procession.
From the volute-krater of Clitias. *c.* 570 BC. Cf. Plate 51 b

Pl. 48b   the proceedings with a meaningful gesture. But Athene, Hermes and Thetis are also observers of Achilles' fatal
passion. The painter cannot do enough to link the Olympian and earthly spheres.

     The next event from the life of Achilles is not, as we might at first expect, one of the great scenes from the poem
of the Wrath of Achilles. Not until the later sixth century is art at last ripe for the representation of the anger, love
Pl. 51c   and grief of Achilles. The episode which Clitias has chosen is the funeral-games for Patroclus and thus the pomp
of the other friezes is matched by this hour of greatest brilliance in the life of the hero for, in this festival, Achilles
was the highly honoured focus of the Greek army. We can discern some of the valuable prizes underneath the slender
horses: a cauldron, a tripod, etc. The height of Achilles' glory is quickly followed by his death. On the handles of
the krater, Clitias has twice painted Ajax rescuing the dead Achilles from the battle. One of these representations is
richer, but the other more convincingly depicts the carrying of the body.

     Clitias has less to tell us about Theseus, since, at that time, the epic of the deeds of Theseus did not yet exist.
Fig. 18, Pls. 51a, b   He does not illustrate the long-familiar tale of the slaying of the Minotaur but, instead, depicts the victory-dance
of the liberated youths and maidens on the island of Delos, showing everything, from the ship in which they
arrive—painted with splendid vivacity—to the mistress of the feast, the divine Ariadne. She later becomes the
consort of the god of Wine who, in the main frieze of the krater, appears as the centre of all this painted world.
The theme particularly occupied Athenians at that time, because they were beginning to adhere more to the cult
of the great Ionic temple on Delos and, at the same time, were giving shape to the cult of Dionysus in Athens.
Pl. 50   The frieze of the dance is followed, below, by the victory over the Centaurs of Theseus, Perithous and the rest
Pl. 27c   of the Lapiths. If we compare this with the representation of Caeneus on the bronze relief from Olympia, which
is only two generations older, our surprise at the power which narrative art has meanwhile gained is increased.
Pl. 51b   Admittedly the beautiful forest is now missing, and its divine inhabitants have let their dignity relax into a raging
fury, but this fury has all the grandeur of a thunderstorm. In contrast to the dark-eyed warriors, the Centaurs have
wide-open, staring eyes showing much of the white. The hair of the combatants bristles and streams, arms wield
trees and hurl great white boulders in hostile encounters of every description. There are fights over fallen Centaurs
and there is some bold overlapping, for instance where three Centaurs rush at Caeneus. The ferocity of the scene
is most subtly contrasted with that of the incomparably rich and splendid scene of the ship's arrival: there we are
Pl. 50   nearer to everyday life whilst here we breathe a more heroic air. Further down the vase we have the procession of

62

the Olympians and with this we see how the juxtaposition of the different spheres intensifies the particular significance of each one.

The next scene, which follows below the main frieze, is not a further one from the life of Theseus but shows the return of Hephaestus to Olympus. The Smith-god and Athene were worshipped together in Athens; the Pls. 50, 52 importance of the cult is attested by the 'Hephaesteon' (the so-called 'Theseon') which was built in the city for this pair of gods. But our frieze too honours the worth of Hephaestus among the Olympians and with this the return to Olympus of the Smith-god. The story was probably first told in a Hymn to Hephaestus of the time of Solon, the existence of which we can only infer from the illustrations. Hephaestus was lame from birth. His mother Hera was so ashamed of this deformity that she threw him out of Olympus. But the daughters of Oceanus, or, according to other sources, the inhabitants of Lemnos, received him kindly and, whilst he lived amongst them, he created his artistic works. These included a throne which he sent to his mother Hera. When she sat on it she was bound fast by invisible fetters. One after the other the roused Olympians visited Hephaestus to try to persuade him to release his mother; but they were all ignominiously sent home. Only Dionysus succeeded in the task by making Hephaestus drunk and bringing him back to Olympus in a procession of revellers. The scene on the vase shows Aphrodite, Hephaestus' future wife, waiting before his enthroned parents, Zeus and Hera; the beautiful goddess is recoiling slightly from the strange aspect of the lascivious following. Clitias is one of the first artists to give the male followers of Dionysus, as 'Sileni,' the hindquarters of horses. Hera has raised her hands in joyful greeting but Ares sits restlessly, ready to leap to his feet, for he is jealous of Hephaestus. In front of him the wise goddess Athene points out the significance of the happenings to other gods as they come hurrying up.

The François vase is our most complete source for the epic style of cyclic narrative; it also helps to give a better understanding of other vase-paintings, in which themes from legend are linked together in a similar way, are selected with a particular ethos and depicted with epic vividness and colour. The difference between this narrative style and that of the Colossal High Archaic style is so great that we might wonder whether the age of Clitias should still be Pls. 38–44a included in the High Archaic period. Yet, despite the delicate arrangement of detail, the volume of the forms is still unbroken and they do not yet have the elasticity of articulation or the dramatic quality which characterize forms in the Late Archaic period, beginning c. 560 BC.

It is a remarkable phenomenon—but one which has received scant notice—that such a lively narrative art was generally current c. 580 BC whilst, in the preceding century, narrative had been increasingly suppressed. This switch from the serenity of the Colossal style to the animation of the age of Clitias cannot be explained as an autonomous development within the visual arts. It must be seen against the flowering of epic poetry which is attested c. 600 BC for the Peloponnese, and in the time of Solon and, in particular, of Pesistratus for Athens. The Attic artists were excellent storytellers. When epic recitations began to fascinate the people, Attic painters were incomparably skilful in assimilating their art to the epic style of narration. The attempts of Corinthian craftsmen to imitate Attic models Pl. 44b were usually failures. Figured vase-painting ceases altogether in Corinth c. 550 BC.

Attic vase-paintings not only reveal their closeness to the cyclic epics; they also make manifest the spirit of the age of Solon, especially in their choice of themes. In the legends of the gods it is quite striking how frequently we meet the punishment of wrongdoers. Solon had explained the suffering of man as caused by his presumption and had preached a new ethos. His attitude led to a new and grandiose view, current in Athens at that time, of the war between the gods and the Titans. On a krater of Lydos we see Zeus, accompanied by a great Victory-goddess and Pl. 41b a serpent, wielding his thunderbolt with a mighty action. The view of Zeus in the battle with the Gigantes—illustrations of which begin to occur in large numbers at a rather later date—is quite different. Although little of Lydos' krater has survived we nevertheless gain the impression of a spacious composition dominated by the figures of Zeus and his opponents, whereas the representations of the battle with the Gigantes show Zeus mounting his chariot in the midst of fellow-combatants who are all equally active in the scene.

From *c.* 550 BC the battle between the gods and the armour-clad Gigantes was one of the most popular Attic themes. From time to time it was woven into the peplos, the robe which was presented to Athene at her great festival every four years; the first occasion was probably in the year when the festival was first arranged, 566 BC. The illustrations of the Gigantes—to appear in our next volume—help us to infer something about the original version of the legend as it must have been shown in the first peplos, and this is wholly in the character of the period under discussion. We are reminded of the fights between the gods in the later sections of the *Iliad*.

This period must have seen the creation of a poem about the battle with the Gigantes, possibly forming part of the cyclic epic of the *Titanomachia*. The subtle characterization and differentiation of the gods corresponds exactly to that which we have observed on the François vase. Zeus is the foremost warrior; he is mounting his war-chariot. His nearest companions are Heracles and Athene. Hera restricts her activities to stripping the armour from the vanquished warriors and dealing them the death-blow. Hephaestus is busy bringing pieces of iron to a glowing heat in his forge, and Aphrodite projects these 'incendiary bombs'; but a literary tradition makes the opponent of Hephaestus the only Giant to escape with his life. This demonstrates the Greeks' poor opinion of the effectiveness of such war-machines. The heroic weapons were considered more noble. The Greeks had a high standard of tech-

Fig. 17, Pl. 43 nology but they made extraordinarily little use of it. The fights with Typhon and the Titans had still had the character of an 'aristia', an individual battle of Zeus, but in the battle with the Gigantes all the gods take part, and their opponents are also differentiated. The most affecting incident is Mother Earth's plea for her sons since she, in her mysterious and inexhaustible fertility, is herself the cause of ever new dissension.

When later authors call the Gigantes simply 'giants' and when, from the Late Classical period on, they are given serpent-tails for feet or, even as early as 520 BC, appear in Titanic nakedness in gables in Athens and Delphi, this shows that the Gigantes are no longer distinguished from those other adversaries of gods, Typhon and the Titans. In the original poem of the Gigantes, it is directly obvious that the Gigantes are in no way fantastic figures but, as armour-clad warriors, are in themselves terrifying enough to meet the gods in battle. Equally significant is the fact that the gods can only win with the help of a mortal since every true conflict presupposes powers which are a match for one another. The victory was also linked with the participation of Dionysus because it was just at that time that the god had joined the company of the Olympians. But Athene, goddess of moderation in battle, was considered the true victor. Her great festival, the Panathenaea, was the recurring celebration of the victory over the Gigantes.

Shortly before the establishment of the Panathenaea we find the first evidence in Athens for the image of an armour-clad Athene on Early Attic coins and, soon afterwards, also on the prize-vases awarded to the victors in the contests of the Panathenaea. This brings us into the period of the great poet and statesman, Solon; it was apparently at that time also that the oldest Parthenon was founded, a second temple of Athene besides the one which contained her long-venerated cult-image. The armour-clad image of Athene probably stood in this Parthenon.

Divine battles, as conceived in the spirit of this age, continued to have an influence on rather later representations of such scenes, for instance the fight between Heracles and Cycnus, the son of Ares. The finest of these is a frieze which encircles the oinochoe of the Lydos painter, but the date of its production places this vase in our next volume. Zeus himself has stepped between the combatants to act as arbitrator and other gods are riding up in chariots to help

64

19 Actaeon being torn to pieces by his dogs. Black-figure lip-cup. *c.* 570–560 BC.—Now lost

in the decision. Cycnus had stolen sacrificial animals intended for Apollo. As in the battle with the Gigantes, Heracles is the champion of Olympian order and here, at the same time, opposes Ares, the immoderate spirit of war.

The same attitude determines the portrayal of the punishment of other transgressors at the time of Solon: Niobe had boasted that she had more children than Leto, the mother of Apollo and Artemis; in consequence she has to Pl. 53 witness the death of her children. Actaeon, having offended Artemis—later it was told how, whilst hunting, he had seen her bathing—was torn to pieces by his own hounds. Tityus had tried to violate Leto and was pursued by Apollo Fig. 19 and Artemis. In Polygnotus' Necyia and, later, in the landscapes of the *Odyssey*, we find him as a penitent in Hades where vultures feed on his liver. In early times we see this punishment carried out only on Prometheus, for the Pl. 41a image of the fettered prisoner who is tormented by eagles is linked, in Attic tradition, with Heracles' rescue. Pl. 57a The figure of Prometheus may still therefore be intended. Pandareus, like Tantalus, had misused the friendship of the gods, having stolen a hound of Zeus. It happens that we have a representation of the theft but not of the punishment.

As well as their battles, the assemblies of the gods are now also differently conceived. We have already met the most magnificent of such assemblies on the François vase: the wedding of Peleus and Thetis and the return of Hephaestus. We compared the divine processions of the Early Archaic period with the *Hymn to Apollo* which is Pls. 46, 48a, 50, 52 preserved under the name of Homer. The *Hymn to Hephaestus*, the existence of which Wilamowitz has inferred from Clitias' frieze, must have been richer and more vivid. The *Hymn to Hermes* has survived and this gives us a portrait full of similar humour and variety. It tells how the cunning god, scarcely an hour after his birth, steals the herd of his brother Apollo. On an amphora in Geneva, Yalouris has discovered Hermes amongst a herd of cattle, and rightly interprets the scene as an allusion to this hymn. Other later hymns to gods are also linked with sixt-h century Attic art; the best known example is the bowl of Exekias in Munich. It shows Dionysus after he has changed into dolphins the pirates who were intending to carry him off as booty; he has made vines twine miraculously about the mast and now sails, as a conqueror, over the calm sea.

> Soon strange things   were seen among them.
> First, wine,   fragrant and sweet,
> flowed in streams   through the black ship.
> Wonder seized   the watching crew,
> all were amazed   at the marvellous odour.
> Suddenly a vine   stretched along the sail-top;
> clusters hung down from it,   and dark ivy
> twined round the mast,   teeming with flowers
> and rich with berries;   garlands bedecked
> all the thole-pins.   Those who saw
> ordered the helmsman   to head for land.
> But the God became   a grim lion,
> roaring proudly,   high on the peak;
> and another marvel—   he made a bear,
> shaggy-necked, standing   at the ship's centre.
> It gazed hungrily,   and the lion glared.
> In fear, the sailors   fled to the stern,
> crowding round the helmsman: he only had shown wisdom.
> Suddenly the lion   sprang on the Master.
> The rest all leapt   into the radiant sea,
> fleeing in panic   a miserable fate.
> They became dolphins;   but Dionysus had pity
> and held back the helmsman,   granted him happiness.

Homeric Hymn VII *to Dionysus*, 34–53

Athene's birth from the head of Zeus is now one of the great themes of the sixth century BC; in the Late Archaic period it becomes an occasion for depicting the assembly of the Olympians. In the High Archaic period we know only the concise, compact, highly expressive shield-relief groups which have taken the place of the type of the Early Archaic relief from Tenos with its mysterious quality of variety. Athene makes her appearance fully armed to the hips. Hephaestus, having struck the blow of delivery, turns away towards the right, alarmed by the tremendous sight which, nevertheless, holds his fascinated gaze. But the midwife Eleithyia steadfastly holds the head of Zeus. In the later relief the powerful disharmony of the older one yields to a multipartite epic narrative. Eleithyia, marvelling at the miracle, is no longer touching Zeus, and Athene dominates the scene with the brilliance of her divine manifestation.

The love of the gods is rarely illustrated in the Archaic period, but the most frequently depicted of such scenes

Figs. 20, 21
Pl. 13

66

20 Birth of Athena. Shield-relief. Width of strip 7.4 cm. ($2^{15}/_{16}$ in.). *c.* 600 BC.—Olympia

21 Birth of Athena. Shield-relief. Width of strip 8.6 cm. ($3^{3}/_{8}$ in.). *c.* 580–570 BC.—Olympia

shows Zeus, in the shape of a bull, carrying Europa over the sea. We can compare the serene, Early Archaic version Pl. 11b of the legend with the most magnificent version: the one in the treasury of Cleisthenes of Sicyon in Delphi. As the mighty bull storms along, his head is stretched forward so that Europa is forced to lean far to the front to enable Pl. 55b herself to grasp his horn firmly with her left hand. The effect of tension produced by the animal's muscles, the body and the drapery is the ultimate expression of the power and strength of Archaic art.

Among the heroic legends those of Perseus and Bellerophon, as depicted by High Archaic artists, were discussed in the section on the Colossal style, because the most significant illustrations of these legends belong to the seventh Pls. II, 40b, 44a, 45 century BC. The scenes with Heracles, on the other hand, belong predominantly to the early sixth century. The whole of Heracles' life is now recounted in pictures, but in the manner of the cyclic epics. We might infer, from this, that there existed an epic of 'cyclic' character in which the deeds of Heracles were linked together by the idea of guilt and atonement. Whereas the starting-point of the earlier poem about Heracles (p. 24) had been his all-mastering passion—as also in the poem of the Wrath of Achilles—the focus is now on a lapse for which the hero must atone through his deeds. This is connected with the anger of the jealous Hera.

Heracles was married to Megara, daughter of the Theban king Creon, and he had several children by her. Hera, however, laid a fit of madness on him in which he killed his wife and children. The unhappy man went to Delphi where the Pythia told him that he must serve King Eurystheus for twelve years. If he accomplished all the tasks the latter should set him he would become immortal. We have already seen how he overcomes the Nemean Lion, the Hydra, the Stymphalian Birds, the Centaurs and the Moliones, how he wins the girdle of the Amazon Queen and fights Apollo for the tripod. Many of these themes are now differently conceived. We see him wrestling Fig. 22 with the invulnerable lion which he cannot overpower in any other way and whose pelt he can cut up and flay only with the aid of the lion's own claws. The most important illustrations of the fight with the lion do not appear until the Late Archaic period. The fight with the Hydra is, on the other hand, exceptionally well suited to a colourful type of epic narrative; even the gable of a small building (a treasury?) on the Acropolis has a decoration with this

22 Heracles wrestling with the lion. Shield-relief. Width of strip 7.2 cm. (2¹³/₁₆ in.).
c. 600 BC.—Olympia

Pl. 54a theme. On the left of the scene we see Heracles' companion Iolaus who is looking after the team. The horses have their noses to the ground as they sniff at the giant crab going to the help of the Hydra. The figure of Heracles is given the highest position in the gable. He wields his club against the Hydra which fills the whole of the other half of the gable and whose swarming presence has never been made to appear more sinister.

On Corinthian vases too we quite frequently find representations of the Hydra swarming widely over the surface.
Fig. 23 The master of a skyphos, which is now lost, combines Heracles' fight with the Hydra with his mastering of Cerberus, the Hound of Hell; he thus shows an early and a late deed, two achievements situated at the extremes of the hero's cycle of legends. At roughly the same time as the creation of this vase-painting, the poet of the *Iliad* (V, 395 ff.) makes Heracles combat Hades himself, which explains why we here see Hades fleeing from Heracles. The original meaning of the legend was that Heracles, by this victory, won immortality. By his bold intrusion he is also able to deliver the two friends Theseus and Perithous. The two had, like Heracles, forced their way into the Underworld to bring aid to the Attic goddess Persephone who had been abducted by Hades. But, by magic, Hades had rooted
Fig. 24 the friends to a throne. A shield-relief shows us Heracles as, with drawn sword, he strides towards the entreating

23 Heracles fighting the Hydra and Heracles in Hades. Skyphos from Argos. *c.* 590–580 BC.—Now lost

24 Heracles with Theseus and Perithous in Hades. Shield-relief. Width of strip 6.2 cm. (2⁷/₁₆ in.). c. 580–570 BC.—Olympia

25 Heracles fighting with Geryon. Shield-relief. Width of strip 8.6 cm. (3³/₈ in.). c. 570–560 BC.—Olympia

prisoners, determined to deliver the unhappy men by force. It was not until the fifth century that the legend received its new form in which Theseus alone is released without Perithous.

In our inferred cyclic poem of Heracles, the hero repeatedly attains the uttermost limits of achievement. If some bronze shield-reliefs, which show a fleeing, unarmed daemon characterized by shaggy hair and hideous features, have been correctly interpreted, he even conquers old age. But the feat which brought Heracles his greatest glory was his delivery of Prometheus, as told in the *Theogony* of Hesiod. The fact that Peloponnesian art knows only the torture of Prometheus, whilst his delivery at the hands of Heracles is known only to Attic artists, substantiates the long-standing supposition that these lines of the *Theogony* were a later interpolation. This linking of the figures of Heracles and Prometheus does, at any rate, remind us that another Attic poet had woven Heracles into the legend of the Gigantes: we cannot mistake the cyclic intention of linking the different cycles of legends in a meaningful combination. For a study of the krater it was necessary to reconstruct the fragments which, fine though they were, were difficult to make out in detail; in the reconstruction, the figure of the archer, to the left of the fettered prisoner, was made clearly recognizable. The huge eagle is already bleeding from a wound inflicted by one of Heracles' arrows. The fearsome beak is open as the bird gasps for its last few breaths. The scene is framed by creatures of the wild. Pl. 57b Pl. 57a

There are traces which suggest that, in this period, there also existed illustrations of Heracles bringing the captured Erymanthian Boar to Eurystheus who, terrified, hides inside a jar; there were also portrayals of Heracles wrestling with Apollo for possession of the tripod. Representations of the fight with the triple-bodied giant Geryon have survived better. Guardian of a marvellous herd of cattle in the land of the gods far to the west, he was the son of Chrysaor and therefore the grandson of Medusa. He was originally a daemon of death. Like Hades he is the owner of cattle; in one version of the Cerberus-legend it is another of Heracles' tasks to steal the cattle of Hades. We are reminded of the shamanic journeys, of the winning of the Golden Fleece. Geryon, like Hades again, has a fearsome dog as companion. Heracles kills this dog, Orthrus, as well as the herdsman Eurytion, before doing battle with Geryon. The artist of the shield-relief sacrifices these motifs to the concentrated portrayal of close combat. As Heracles presses forward with drawn sword and outstretched left arm the two assailants come to close quarters. Geryon, wearing full hoplite-armour, rushes to the attack with fixed spears, but the nearest of the three warriors is already stricken—his head has fallen back and his arms hang slack. Fig. 25, Pl. 77

69

After the victory over Geryon, Heracles is promised immortality with the completion of one further task to be imposed by Eurystheus: the winning of the golden apples of the Hesperides. Like Geryon the guardians of the tree of Paradise live in the extreme west. Heracles can find out the way there only from Nereus, the wise and kindly Sea-god whose knowledge has to be won from him by a hard wrestling-match. Only such beings as Nereus, who are proof against the deadly destructiveness of the ocean, know the way to the land of the gods. Later artists show the hero wrestling with Triton—a closely related being—whilst the august Nereus looks on. The period under discussion has produced nothing which can be definitely identified as an illustration of the actual obtaining of the apples, but the representation of the fight with Triton, in the gable of the ancient Temple of Athene on the Acropolis at Athens, is worthy to stand beside the older gable of Corfu as one of the most important works of the Archaic period.

The centre of the gable on the Temple of Athene was probably occupied by the group—which has survived in large sections—of two lions felling a bull; this is a powerful natural image which bears witness to the might of the goddess as does the Gorgon in the gable of the Corfu temple. The master of the Athenian gable is comparing the action of the hero (who is constantly under Athene's protection) with the natural image in the centre. But he depicts his scenes with greater warmth, variety and colour than does the Corfu master, and his portrayals have a ballad-like richness. The Old Man of the Sea, holding in his hands symbols for fire, water and air, has three bodies as a sign of his faculty of shape-shifting; he is also winged. The complicated coils of the serpent-body contrast with the powerful fish-body of Triton which meanders in flat curves, as well as with the strongly muscled body of the hero which seems, similarly, to writhe out from the corner of the gable. This is no life-and-death struggle; Triton and the Old Man of the Sea will come to no harm and Heracles will be a step nearer immortality. The work therefore has an air of gaiety and cheerful *joie de vivre*. This is matched by the painting in strong, glowing colours which have lasted better on the limestone than they do on sculptures in marble. Here, more than in vase-paintings or shield-reliefs, we are able to gain some idea of the splendid actuality of legend; we think of the Athenians of the Archaic period whose eyes were daily greeted by this highly accomplished work.

It is clearly the intention to make the hero penetrate every region of the world: under the earth to Hades, westwards to Geryon and the Hesperides, northwards to the Caucasus. In the south he conquers Antaeus—hitherto not represented on High Archaic monuments—and in the east the Amazons. In the period of the epic renaissance, artists are fond of elaborating this last-mentioned theme, which we met in the scene of single combat on the Tiryns shield, into complex battle-scenes.

The epic about the deeds of Heracles presumably also incorporated the earlier one, whose existence we have inferred, dealing with his amorous passion. The representations of Heracles carrying off Deianeira as his bride, fighting with the Centaur Nessus and first encountering Iole are some of the most powerful of the surviving High Archaic works.

More clearly than hitherto, we now see the maturity of narrative art in these scenes; they are no longer based simply on a splendid presentiment, as in Early Archaic times, but on a knowledge of the emotions and moods of the human heart. This applies not only to Heracles' awakening love for Iole and her fearful hesitation; to Deianeira's last look into the eyes of her mother; and to the uneasiness of the father and the impetuous boldness of Heracles in the departure-scene; but also to the struggle between Heracles and Nessus. The Centaur is now a less noble figure than in several Early Archaic versions of the incident. His nose is blunt and coarse and his beard is untidy; he is screaming basely and plaintively begs Heracles to spare his life as the hero's left foot lands in the small of his back

Pl. 55a
Pls. 56a, b

Fig. 16

Pl. 56

Pl. 58a

Pls. 57c, 59, 60a, III

III Heracles catching sight of Iole at the banquet of Eurytus. Corinthian krater. Height 46 cm. (18¹/₈ in.). *c.* 600 BC.—Paris. Cf. Plate 60a

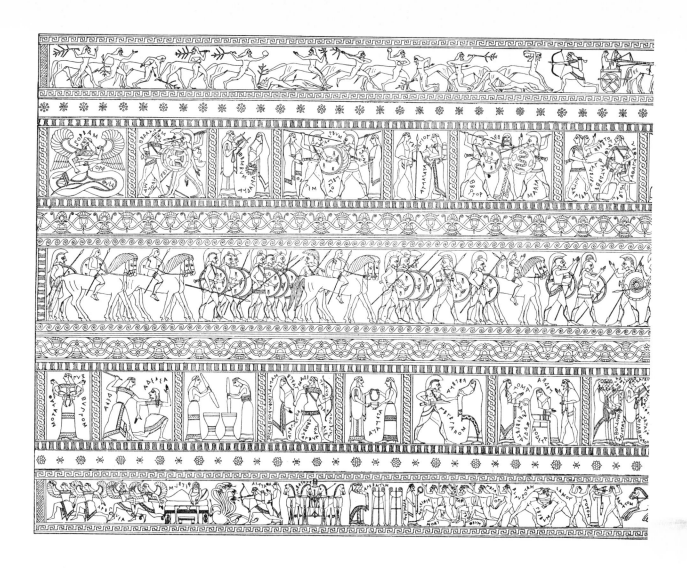

26   The Chest of Cypselus. *c.* 570 BC.—Reconstruction after W. von Massow

Bottom strip (right to left): Pelops and Oenomaus—The departure of Amphiaraus—The funeral-games for Pelias: Heracles and a girl flute-player; the chariot-race; the boxers; the wrestlers; the discus-thrower; the runners; Acastus, prizes and three Peliads—The fight with the Hydra: Iolaus looking after the chariot; Heracles fighting the Hydra; Phineus, Boreads and Harpies. *Second strip (left to right):* Night with Death and Sleep—Dice and Adicia—Women working at mortars—Idas and Marpessa—Zeus and Alcmene—Menelaus and Helen—Marriage of Jason and Medea—Apollo and the choir of Muses—Atlas and Heracles—Ares and Aphrodite—Peleus and Thetis—Two Gorgons and Perseus. *Middle strip:* Frieze of warriors (showing the troops in the style fashionable at the time, *i. e.* with no chariots but with mounted soldiers and with reserve-horses). *Fourth strip (left to right):* Boreas and Oreithyia—Heracles and Geryon—Theseus and Ariadne—Achilles and Memnon—Melanion and Atalanta—Hector and Ajax—The Dioscuri, Helen and Aethra—Coon and Agamemnon—Judgment of Paris—Artemis (as 'Potnia Theron')—Ajax and Cassandra (on the right is Athene)—Eteocles and Polyneices—Dionysus. *Top strip (right to left):* Wedding-night of Peleus and Thetis: The couple on a couch in a cavern—Maids working—The Centaur Cheiron as host in the cave—Hephaestus (left) delivering weapons to the Nereids (two in each of the four chariots) as a wedding-present for Peleus and Thetis—Two women on a mule-drawn carriage—Heracles and the Centaurs.

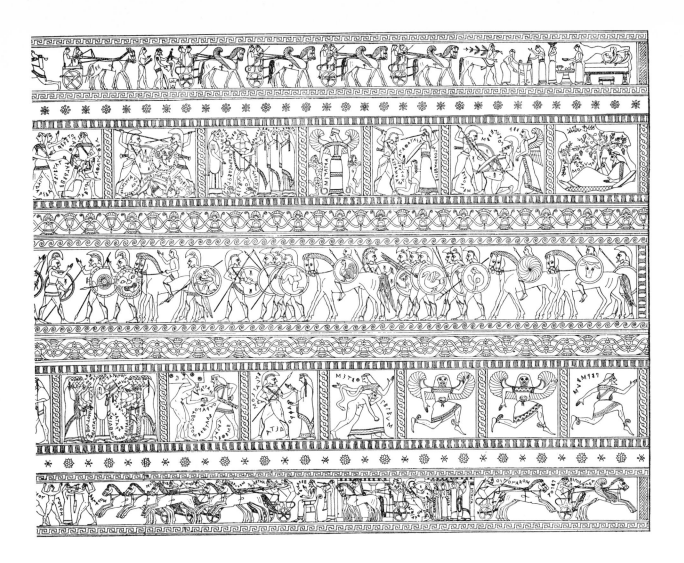

and he grasps Nessus by the hair, threatening to stab him. But, despite the dramatic violence, the forms are even bigger and fuller than in the epic phase of the High Archaic period; we are meant to see the essence of the two characters in their relationship to one another, and this is more important to the painter than the actual episode.

The Middle Corinthian bowl which shows Heracles wrestling with the River-god Achelous belongs to the epic phase. The painter compares this scene with Theseus' fight with the Minotaur, which he has depicted to the left of it. Immediately to the right of the group with Theseus we see the dignified figure of Deianeira's father, followed by the closely entwined group of the wrestlers, and then the figure of the bride in front of the chariot in which Heracles is to carry her off. The figure of a running spear-bearer is unidentifiable. The type of the narrative, with its suggestion of the style of a picture-book, reveals that the connections between the stories have become more important than a profound conception of the episode itself. This explains the wealth of closely-packed ornament and other motifs, such as serpents and birds, which are interwoven with the action giving something of the effect of a tapestry.

In addition to the deliberate enterprises of Heracles there are others into which he is forced by accident. One of

Pl. 58b

27 Theseus fighting with the Minotaur. Shield-relief. Width of strip 7.2 cm. (2¹³/₁₆ in.). *c.* 600 BC.—Olympia

these—which we have already met—is his adventure with the Centaurs of Pholoe who were attracted by the scent

Pl. 62 of wine. A Middle Corinthian scyphus shows Pholus looking on in amazement as Heracles, who has had no time to reach for his weapons, chases away the Centaurs with firebrands. The benevolent spirits Athene and Hermes, who have been waiting and feasting for so long outside the cave until Heracles should have finished his meal, also watch the wonderful deed with astonishment. In even lighter vein is the adventure with the Cercopes, imps who try to

Pl. 61a steal the hero's weapons. One of the best-preserved of the shield-reliefs shows how Heracles has hung the rascals up by the bend of their knees without actually binding them, so that the contrast between the hero and these miserable wretches, with their threshing arms, is made all the more obvious. This well-preserved fragment gives us the best impression of the fine compositional art in this type of relief.

The 'cyclic' narrative of the deeds of Heracles was probably matched by a work in which the story was told in simple pictorial form especially for the barbarians who did not know Greek. We must assume the existence of such 'picture-books' in order to understand the familiarity of the Etruscans with Greek legend; the fact that Italian monuments occasionally show the events in sequence would also fit the inference. To us it seems obvious that a story should be told in sequence, yet in none of our illustrations hitherto examined have we found this so obvious feature (cf. p. 97).

In their metope-reliefs, vase-paintings and shield-reliefs the Greeks liked to combine poetico-mythological analogies from various legend-cycles instead of choosing a particular legend and telling the story in its correct

Pl. 58b sequence. A deed of Heracles is, for instance, placed opposite one of Theseus. We find this same manner of combining motifs in literature, *e.g.* in the odes of Pindar and in the choral odes of the tragedies. Narrative series of pictures evidently existed in picture-book form, for we find copies of such pictorial narratives on Hellenistic relief-decorated vases. In monumental art, however, the other principle prevailed.

Fig. 26 The scenes on the celebrated 'Ark of Cypselus' were also arranged in this way. This valuable, relief-decorated work is known to us only from Pausanias' description, but, from our knowledge of contemporary vases of a similar type, we can, to a certain extent, imagine for ourselves the appearance of the pictures on the chest and so date the work to *c.* 570 BC. The ark may have been made for Olympia by the family of the Cypselidae who were in exile at that time, in the same way as the exiled Attic Alcmaeonidae distinguished themselves by setting up great institu-

Pl. 64b tions in Delphi. The dating is also supported by the finding in Delphi, in 1939, of similar reliefs which are datable

to *c.* 570 BC. The significance behind the combination of the funeral-games for Pelias with the departure of Amphiaraus, in the bottom strip on the chest, will shortly be seen. In the second strip from the lower half, the scenes are concerned with the love-suits of gods and heroes; the central piece is a wedding and all the conflicts end in reconciliation. The fourth strip contains battle-scenes which alternate with peaceful scenes whilst, above, we see Cheiron with other Centaurs. The meaning behind the combinations of themes is often obscure.

In contrast to the treatment of the story of Heracles this period illustrates few incidents from that of Theseus; it is a popular practice to associate scenes from the story of Theseus with some of the deeds of Heracles. We saw how Heracles'   Pl. 58b fight with Achelous was combined with Theseus' battle with the Minotaur; there are also three shield-reliefs in which the last-mentioned scene is shown together with Heracles' fight   Fig. 22 with the lion. We have already met the impressive scene in which Heracles encounters Theseus and Perithous in Hades.   Fig. 24 When looked at beside the compactness of these scenes, the breadth in the portrayal of the dance on Delos and the battle   Pls. 50, 51 with the Centaurs on the François vase is all the more unusual and significant in its effect. On the Ark of Cypselus, Theseus and Ariadne were portrayed—again evidently during the victory-celebrations—facing each other and holding a lyre and a wreath respectively. One of the forerunners of this scene is a relief, recently discovered, on the leg of a tripod from Olympia. With his left hand, Theseus fingers the strings of the   Fig. 28 lyre; a band, with the plectron, hangs on his lower-arm. He is bearded and wears a short, girdled chiton. Ariadne—standing with greater composure—is clad in a simple, long girdled chiton with decorated borders as its only adornment. Her thick hair, parted over her shoulders, is held together by a ribbon only, at the nape of her neck. She has raised her left arm in glad greeting. With their right hands both of them hold the wreath which had shed light in the darkness of the

28 Tripod-leg from Olympia: Mistress of the Animals; Theseus and Ariadne; legation to Achilles; Achilles slaying Troilus. Length 1.21 m. (47⁵/₈ in.). *c.* 600 BC.—Olympia

Labyrinth. We can admire the warmth of life in this representation even 'more if we compare it with earlier illus-

Pl. 27a trations of meetings, such as Theseus' first wooing of Ariadne.

Pl. 5c, Fig. 33   The abduction of Helen, an incident which we met in the Early Archaic period, occurs in a refined new version
Pl. 80 on shield-reliefs. Theseus, who wins the love of the Amazon Antiope, may be the subject of a bronze relief from
Olympia in the Ionian style of Magna Graecia. In it we see a warrior grasping, with his right hand, the knee of
Pl. 28 a female warrior as she rushes towards him—this recalls the scene of Peleus and his beloved Thetis; the woman has
placed her right hand on his chin in a gesture of entreaty. Behind her we see a woman—probably the goddess
Aphrodite—unveiling herself. This scene differs so utterly from the spirit of representations of the Penthesilea-story
that we must obviously seek some other Amazon who was opposed and loved by a warrior: the couple can be no
other than Antiope and Theseus. After becoming King of Athens, Theseus is forced to defend his kingdom against
a wild army of women; similarly Achilles has to do battle against an army of women outside Troy. Theseus had
accompanied Heracles on the latter's campaign against the Amazons and had won their queen Antiope for his wife;
she was later to bear him his son Hippolytus. The Amazons, seeking revenge for the abduction of their queen,
attacked Athens. In the hard defensive battle Antiope fell, but Theseus succeeded in gaining a victory over the army
of the Amazons. Our next volume will show that the great epic on the subject of the deeds of Theseus was not
created until the late sixth century BC. Individual features of the legend could, however, be older, and these may
be contained in scenes such as the one on our bronze relief.

        Theseus' abduction of Helen leads us to the *Cypria*. But in the period we are discussing we find a whole cycle
of legend-illustrations which take their place between the cycles of the deeds of Heracles and Theseus and that of
the Trojan War; from these illustrations we can infer the existence of a great epic—possibly a Corinthian one—
Pl. 47 datable to *c.* 600 BC. We have shown the pictorial form given by Attic artists to the Hunt of the Calydonian boar
Pls. 60b, 61b in the François vase, but we can also see a rather earlier version on a bowl of quite uncommon monumentality. On
the larger of the fragments we can discern the boar surrounded by attacking and dying dogs whilst Antaeus writhes
on the ground in his death-agony. The hero who kneels, on the left, in front of the monster and plunges his spear
into the boar's throat is wearing only one shoe; this hero may, therefore, be Jason whom we shall meet in the legend
of the Argonauts, as the hero with only one shoe. There are two arrows stuck in the boar's hindquarters, and now
Atalanta enters the scene as an archer; she comes from the right, not, as in the François vase, from the left. Her figure
is preserved on the smaller of the vase's fragments, striding out with a powerful step and once more bending her
bow. Behind her back we can discern the hand and spear of another huntsman, but only the ending of his name
(—os) remains, behind Atalanta's head. This could be Meleager, in which case the attacking huntsman, whose back
view we see in front of Atalanta, is most likely to be Melanion. The grouping of the huntsmen thus differs very
much from that on the François vase and could be closer to the original pictorial invention. Clitias' arrangement
of his pairs of huntsmen does, certainly, give an impressive collective picture of the hunt, but the individual heroes
are not so well characterized as in the original motifs which we find on the fragments of the bowl.

        In High Archaic art the Hunt of the Calydonian boar is frequently linked with the funeral-games held by the
Fig. 26 Argonauts, after their return, in honour of old Pelias, and the funeral-games are, in turn, connected with the departure of Amphiaraus. Many heroes take part in all three enterprises. It therefore seems likely that some epic, in which
all three are linked, underlies the combination of the episodes in art. The throne of Jason's father, Aeson, King of
Iolcus, was usurped by his cousin Pelias, who then ruled Iolcus himself. Jason's mother therefore brought her son to
the Centaur Cheiron to be reared. When he reached manhood Jason set off for Iolcus. On the way an old woman

76

asked him to carry her across a swollen river. After he had helped her she revealed herself as the goddess Hera who, from then on, became his patroness. In crossing the river Jason had lost a sandal in the mud; Pelias was greatly alarmed when he saw him, for an oracle had warned him against a man with only one shoe. To rid himself of anxiety he set Jason the apparently impossible task of fetching the Golden Fleece from Colchis.

The wonderful ram, which the Fleece had originally clothed, had been sent by Nephele (the Cloud) to her children Phrixus and Helle when they were being persecuted by their treacherous stepmother. The ram was to carry the children over the sea to Colchis. But over the Hellespont—the straits to which she has given her name—Helle failed to hold fast and fell into the sea, where she became a Nereid. At the end of his journey Phrixus sacrificed the ram and became the father of a flourishing line. To reach Colchis Jason, with Hera's help, built the first large ship, the Argo, into which he set a piece of the sacred oak of Dodona which had the gift of speech. Then he called together fifty of the noblest heroes of Greece, some of whom, like himself and the Dioscuri, had already taken part in the Calydonian Hunt. In many cases they are, like Peleus, fathers of some of the heroes who are later to march against Troy. This company was joined by Heracles and by Orpheus, the wonderful singer whose song brought together wild and tame creatures in peaceful union and could even move woods and mountains. One of the magnificent metopes of the ancient treasury of the Sicyonians in Delphi shows one half of the Argo; it is framed by the figures Pl. 63a of the Dioscuri who ride through the air and are therefore not standing in the ship. In this metope all the heroes, together with their horses, are represented in full-face because of the uniqueness of the event. The bows of the Argo are, however, carefully portrayed in profile showing the round holes for the oars and the shields hanging from the rail. The lyre-player in the centre is designated by the name of Orpheus—this constitutes the first known portrait of a poet. To his left is the figure of a second minstrel, but no trace has survived of the third hero whom we must assume was also in the picture and who may have been the sharp-eyed pilot Lynceus. It seems that the other half of the Argo was contained in a lost metope. All the surviving metopes of the treasury can be interpreted from this epic combination. For the cyclic narrative style this building is as valuable in providing evidence as is the François vase.

The only one of the many adventures of the Argonauts to be represented in this period is the one in which the sons of the Wind-god Boreas, who are also members of the expedition, chase away the Harpies who every day stole the food of the blind King Phineus, so that he was almost starved to death. In gratitude, Phineus advises them on the best way to pass the greatest obstacle of their voyage, the Symplegades, or clashing rocks; his advice is to follow the example of a dove flying through. On the bowl from Aegina, which we have already met in our discussion of the Perseus legend, the figures of the Boreads are not preserved, but we have what are probably representations of the fleeing Harpies, their hurrying gait and clutching hands expressively differentiated. Pl. 64a

The story is told in more epic style in the ivory relief from Delphi, which gives the best idea of the style of the Ark of Cypselus. On the left of the picture we can make out the hand of Phineus as he reclines on a dining-couch; Pl. 64b beside the hand is one of the King's female companions who appears to be telling him of the wonderful chase. The fine differentiation of pursuers and pursued, all of whom, in their strange realism, are looking out of the picture, is made with Corinthian finesse, delicacy and accuracy. Among the neighbouring scenes we can recognize the departure of Amphiaraus.

In Colchis, Jason won the Fleece with the aid of the sorceress Medea, daughter of the Sun-god. She left her home in order to marry Jason. When, after many wanderings, the Argo finally reached home, Medea gave false advice to the daughters of Pelias, on how to rejuvenate their father. To make her advice plausible, she boiled an old ram in a cauldron into which she had put rejuvenating herbs. The ram emerged as a young he-lamb. When the daughters

of Pelias tried to do the same with their father, however, he died because they had not used the correct herbs. But the
Argonauts organized magnificent funeral-games for Pelias, and these games began to be very frequently represented
in art as being one of the most brilliant manifestations of the community of the Argonauts. To our present-day way
of thinking Medea's trickery is incompatible with the funeral-games and, in actual fact, the illustrations of the bath
of rejuvenation do not appear until rather later. Yet the combining of the two episodes may not have seemed
offensive to the creator of the ancient epic, since Jason had, after all, played no part in the murder of Pelias and he
was also becoming increasingly estranged from the sorceress Medea. The honour of the funeral-games is accorded
to Pelias because he himself was originally celebrated in an individual poem.

Pls. 65, IV

It is on an Attic bowl from the Acropolis that we have the richest portrayal of the funeral-games; unfortunately
this consists only of two groups of adjoining fragments and a further isolated fragment. In one of the groups of
fragments we see, on the left, Peleus and Atalanta wrestling. The two wrestlers do not yet face each other as in later
art, but are placed parallel like Heracles and the lion in early illustrations of that fight. Atalanta wears a short, richly
patterned chiton and a red girdle; her skin is reproduced in white. To each side there must have originally been
densely packed groups of seated and standing heroes looking on, this being a bold, new attempt on the part of the
artist to master the difficulties of a crowd-scene. Only the group on the right survives. All the men wear the dignified
dress of chiton and cloak; almost all are bearded and wear a taenia as adornment. The light skin-colour of the second-
to-last hero on the right was chosen simply for the sake of variety. Only Atalanta's fight receives general attention;
otherwise the fights here seem to be more loosely arranged than in the other group of fragments. Above the tripod—
one of the prize-gifts—on the left of the picture, is the arm of a javelin-thrower. Two heroes await their turn. To
their right we see Melanion, designated by an inscription. He has already made his throw and now meets Amphiaraus, who is on his way to the pitch. A flute-player makes music to accompany the contest; he is followed by Capa-
neus, a hero whom we know from the battle of the Seven against Thebes.

Pl. 65b

Pl. 65a

The fight of Peleus and Atalanta is depicted with greater maturity on a Chalcidian hydria datable to c. 550 BC.
Here the two are facing one another, each grasping the other by the lower-arm. One strange feature of the painting
is the background which is formed by the pelt of the Calydonian boar, as though the games were taking place
immediately after the slaying of the boar. The painter is trying to concentrate the two themes into a single, impressive
scene which was more important to him than any chronological differentiation of the events. The warm and colourful portrayal is Ionian. The dramatic concentration in the composition is already Late Archaic in character.

Pl. IV

King Cleisthenes of Sicyon, who founded the treasury in Delphi bearing the metopes of the Argonauts, was
concerned with other combinations of legends. We know from other sources that, instead of the legends which
were popular in the neighbouring city of Argos (mainly the Trojan ones), he gave preference to new themes which
had never before been represented and which now appear in his treasury. The powerful metope showing the boar
was probably flanked by two others in which the Calydonian huntsmen were shown rushing at the boar. Only
one fragment of a metope of the Phrixus story has survived, and we have already met the metope with Europa on
the bull. There is, in addition, a unique group containing the two pairs of brothers: the Dioscuri and the Apharetids.

Pl. 63a

Pl. 55b

Pl. 63b

Like their sister Helen, the Dioscuri had Zeus as father and Leda as mother; in addition Leda bore her husband
Tyndareus Clytaemnestra, the future wife of Agamemnon. The figures of Helen and Clytaemnestra link the legend
firmly with the Trojan War, but the Dioscuri link it with the earlier story of the expedition of the Argonauts. The
Dioscuri were on friendly terms with the sons of King Aphareus of Messene, who were named Idas and Lynceus.
On the metope we see the four friends on their way home with a herd of stolen cattle (only three of which are

IV Peleus and Atalanta wrestling at the funeral-games for Pelias. Chalcidian hydria. Height 46 cm. (18¹/₈ in.). *c.* 550 BC.—Munich

29 The Sphinx surprising youths. Bowl of the C Painter. Height 14.8 cm. (5⁷/₈ in.). *c.* 570–560 BC.—Syracuse

shown in the picture). Later the pairs of brothers quarrel over some booty or over the daughters of Leucippus, Phoebe and Hilaeira. In the ensuing fight Castor and both of the Apharetids perish. In view of these future events, with which every beholder of the metope would have been familiar, this portrayal of youthful vigour and harmony must have appeared all the more affecting.

Fig. 26   On the Ark of Cypselus, as well as on Attic, Corinthian and Etruscan vases, the funeral-games for Pelias are linked
Pl. 67a with the departure of Amphiaraus, a noble seer who, like Asclepius, later became a god of healing. As we saw above, the Delphic ivory reliefs show, besides the Boreads, also the departure of Amphiaraus who had taken part in the Calydonian Hunt and the expedition of the Argonauts as a hero. Now, however, he became fatefully entangled.
Fig. 29 At Thebes, Oedipus had killed the Sphinx which was destroying the youths of Thebes, who were unable to solve her riddle. As conqueror of the Sphinx, Oedipus was rewarded with the throne of Thebes and the hand of Iocaste. He married her without knowing that she was his mother, and neither did he know that her husband Laius, whom

30 Matricide of Alcmaeon. Tyrrhenian amphora. *c.* 570–560 BC.—Berlin

he had unsuspectingly slain in anger, was his father; Laius had refused to make way for him in the narrow defile on the way to Delphi.

A dreadful fate follows for him and for his descendants. After discovering the truth, Oedipus puts out his own eyes, whilst Iocaste hangs herself. The sons of Oedipus, Eteocles and Polyneices, quarrel over the throne. Polyneices is exiled but he wins the aid of King Adrastus of Argos, who solicits the support of five more heroes, among them Amphiaraus. The latter goes, indeed, under constraint because, as a seer, he foresees the utter failure of the enterprise. But he has promised his wife Eriphyle that he will grant her a wish, and she, having been bribed by Polyneices with a work of Hephaestus, the wonderful necklace of Harmonia, daughter of Aphrodite, induced Amphiaraus to join the expedition. He, however, imposes on his son Alcmaeon the duty of avenging him on his mother.

On the great Corinthian krater we immediately recognize the powerful figure of the seer as he mounts his chariot, drawing his sword and looking round menacingly; for the last of the line of women in the picture is Eriphyle, who is holding the great necklace. The foremost of the figures, however, is Alcmaeon who, like the women behind him, raises his arms imploringly towards his father. Only Eriphyle stands unmoved. Behind the group of figures we can see the façade of the palace and, to the right behind the horses, that of the courtyard-gate, the 'propylon'. Sitting on the ground on the right of the picture, in the attitude befitting a seer, is Halimedes who holds his sceptre in his left hand; full of dire premonitions he clutches with his right hand at the hair on his bowed head. In place of the old filling-ornament we see serpents, eagles and all kinds of other creatures of evil omen, surrounding the central action. The hedgehog is an ancient symbol used for warding off evil. In contrast to the scenes on the François vase, the action is here given dramatic concentration. Moments of significance are combined in a single scene. Yet contemporary Attic artists would show less detail and would subordinate the subsidiary motifs, although, here too, the iron thread of Fate, which none can escape, is conceived with uncanny power. The funeral-games for Pelias on the reverse of the vase, a graphic representation of a crowd-scene, are intended as relief.

One important Attic painter's simplified and concentrated version of the theme can be seen in the painting on a Tyrrhenian amphora. Once again we see an armour-clad warrior mounting his chariot and looking round; this time the warrior is Alcmaeon, the son of Amphiaraus. To the left of him is the funeral-mound of his father and, over it, Fig. 30 the great, majestic figure of Eriphyle has collapsed: Alcmaeon has avenged his father upon her, and now the blood spurts up from her throat. She had come, with her women, to the tomb, feigning grief for Amphiaraus, and there her son had surprised her. Behind her and the tomb a huge snake rises, its jaws gaping menacingly at Alcmaeon; this is probably his mother's avenging spirit. A second Fury—this time in human shape—runs up from the right accompanied by Apollo, who is to absolve Alcmaeon. The painter is fond of the archaic magnificence of richly embroidered robes which, on the figure of the Fury, have a particularly strange effect.

Before the battle at Thebes, the barbarous Tydeus, father of Diomedes, was sent ahead into the city to announce the demands of Polyneices. This is probably the occasion of an incident which, among others, we know of through a Corinthian vase-painting: we see Tydeus rushing, with drawn sword, at Ismene, the daughter of Oedipus, because Pl. V she had been making love with the 'Argonaut' Periclymenus. The coward flees, with great bounds, to the left; his slack bearing contrasts him to the powerful figure of Tydeus, but otherwise the two figures correspond almost symmetrically. The unusual white skin-colour of the 'playboy' links him compositionally with Ismene. On his way back from Thebes, Tydeus fell into an ambush of fifty Thebans, but he killed all except one, whom he sent back as a messenger.

The incomplete nature of our literary sources is demonstrated by the fact that yet another significant scene is

31 Lycurgus and Amphiaraus fighting in front of Adrastus. Attachment-plate of shield-strip 8. Width of strip 7.2 cm. (2¹³/₁₆ in.). *c.* 570–560 BC.—Olympia

Fig. 31   known to us only through shield-reliefs and through a Spartan vase-painting. This is the fight between Amphiaraus and Lycurgus who had to be separated by their commander, Adrastus. In the relief we see Amphiaraus pressing in upon Lycurgus, whilst the other five heroes, King Adrastus in the centre, attempt to separate the furious men. We can imagine how Lycurgus had insulted Amphiaraus, suggesting that his hesitation to take part in the battle was due to cowardice. Like many other heroes, he had thus offended a seer. If this was the case, the story would then be another of the many known to us in which the downfall of the Seven is based on their evil hearts, only the good and religious Amphiaraus being excepted. The rhythmic arrangement of the composition and the individual figures shows that this work, like the other Amphiaraus-scenes just examined, was produced at the very beginning of the Late Archaic period.

In the assault of the Seven on the seven gates of Thebes, the fallen included all the attackers except Adrastus; they also included the mutually hostile brothers Eteocles and Polyneices who killed each other in single combat. Their sister Antigone was killed by King Creon for attempting to bury Polyneices. Amphiaraus, together with his horses, was swallowed up by the earth, later to re-emerge on the surface as a god in his sanctuary at Oropus. None of these happenings are represented in the early period.

We find no illustrations of scenes from the legend-cycle of the Calydonian Hunt, the Argonauts and the Seven against Thebes, until the High Archaic period. The legend of Troy, on the other hand, appears as early as the Late Geometric period. Early Archaic art already contains most of the Trojan themes which we are to meet again now in High Archaic times. But they have been characteristically adapted and made to fit into connected epic groups as in the cycles on the François vase. On the Chigi vase, Paris had calmly awaited the goddesses whose beauty he was Pl. 67b   to judge. But on the early amphora of Lydos in Florence, and in other contemporary paintings, he flees in horror in face of the superhuman apparitions; Hermes is forced to hurry after him, with great strides, to inform him of his task. He tells him that Athene promises him victory and heroism and Hera the overlordship of Europe and Asia, but that Aphrodite promises the possession of the most beautiful of women, Helen, the daughter of Zeus. It is no longer a young prince who must make the decision as in the earlier version. Paris is now bearded and, dressed in chiton and cloak, appears as an august king. An eagle flies significantly ahead of him, whilst the owl of Athene, its great eyes looking out at us from between the legs of Hermes, could be an omen of the future in which Athene is

82

V   Tydeus slaying Ismene because of her love for Periclymenus. From a Corinthian amphora. Height 32 cm. (12⁵/₈ in.). *c.* 560 BC.—Paris

to lead the Greeks to victory. At all events, the disparity between gods and men is now consciously felt as it never
was in earlier art; we are again reminded of the ethos, taught by Solon at that time, by which new weight was
given to the legends about the enemies of the gods.

Many bad men are rich and many good men are poor,
   but we will not exchange goodness and virtue for wealth;
wealth may belong to me now, but it soon may pass to another,
   but from those who possess it goodness will never depart.

. . .

Wealth I desire to possess, but would not have it unjustly;
   Justice is always at hand: vengeance will come from the Gods.

SOLON

Helen was the cause of the Trojan War and her figure reappears in every phase of the legend. It is therefore natural
that a period which liked to enquire into the connections between things should give form to an especially large
number of scenes from the life of Helen. We are already familiar with her abduction by Theseus and her rescue
by the Dioscuri. It is only recently that we learned, from a newly found inscription, that a frequent type of shield-
relief alludes to the betrothal of Menelaus and Helen. All heroes who were later to fight at Troy for the sake of
Helen had, at some time, paid court to her; only Agamemnon, who had already won Clytaemnestra, wooed Helen
on behalf of his younger brother Menelaus. On the relief, however, Menelaus himself, his sceptre in his left hand,
steps up to the bride with a decisive tread and, as befits the chosen husband, clasps her by the left wrist. She expresses
her joy by raising her right hand; her only adornment is a taenia set in her rich hair. The clay relief from Tarentum
showed us Theseus wooing Ariadne: the first meeting and the response. On the bronze relief the wooing has become
a betrothal and the mood of shyness has turned into something of greater warmth and maturity.

These later illustrations show how we may interpret the very much more powerful scene on the funerary stela
in Sparta which had hitherto remained a mystery. Menelaus has put his arm about Helen's shoulders whilst she
hands him the wreath destined for the son-in-law of Zeus *(Hyginus* 78). On the other side of the stela we see Helen
after the conquest of Troy; now wearing the solemn dress of a matron, being threatened with the sword by Menelaus.
Hissing serpents of death rear up the other two sides of the column. Why scenes from the story of Menelaus and
Helen should have been carved on the dead man's funerary monument as parallels to his own life we cannot tell,
but we can admire the simplicity and forcefulness with which the two apparently so similar groups are differentiated:
the calm bearing of the suitor and the vehemence of the avenger, the loose hair of the bride and the veiled head of
the mature woman are merely the most obvious contrasts. Genuinely Spartan features are the length of the legs
and the shortness of the upper-bodies and also the passion expressed within the action.

On shield-reliefs, besides the wooing of Helen, we also find representations of her abduction by Paris. Helen, as
mistress of the house whose treasures she takes with her to Troy, is holding the spindle. Her abductor has drawn
his sword, as he must be on guard against any of Menelaus' men. The large number of such scenes occurring on
shield-bands seems to exalt the person of Helen to such an extent that the Trojan War appears more as a poem about
the divinely beautiful Helen than as a poem about Achilles. The figure of Helen is similarly prominent on the kraters
from Corinth, which are artistically close to the shield-bands. In one such, the wedding of Paris and Helen occupies

Pls. 53, 54b

Figs. 9, 10

Fig. 32

Pl. 27a

Pl. 68
Pl. 69

Pl. 57b
Fig. 33

84

32 Menelaus wooing Helen. Shield-relief. Width of strip 7.3 cm. (2⁷/₈ in.). c. 590–580 BC. Olympia

33 Paris abducting Helen. Shield-relief. Width of strip 7.2 cm. (2¹³/₁₆ in.). c. 600 BC.— Olympia

a whole frieze and, even in the scene of Hector's departure, Paris and Helen are present as a couple. In the wedding-frieze, Paris ('Alexandros') and Helen drive together in a four-horse chariot, most richly clad in colourful chitons and cloaks. Helen is drawing her cloak back from her face in order to greet another couple. We might expect this couple to be Paris' parents, Priam and Hecabe, but the man bears the name of the charioteer Automedon and the other inscription can possibly be reconstructed as Cassandra. As a maiden, she wears no veil. The painter may have consciously opposed the bridal pair with Cassandra, the prophetess who is aware of the coming disaster and who is herself to be the victim of Clytaemnestra. Of less ominous significance are the other groups in which Trojans, in festive garb, take pleasure in their lovely young girl companions. Hippomedon, on the right of the picture, has actually placed his hand on his companion's hip. Hector is also there behind Paris. The other names allude more generally to the war and to Troy, to fighting horses and the deaths of men; even the Gorgon-head on the shield of the warrior on the right is an indication of the coming war.

Pls. 70a, 71b

Pl. 32c

At the time when Menelaus was wooing Helen, Peleus had already won Thetis. It is only after taking part in the Calydonian Hunt and the expedition of the Argonauts, that he is truly worthy of her. One Corinthian krater shows Peleus lying in wait for Thetis beside an altar and a sacred tree. Her divine sisters, the Nereids, flee with a colourful diversity of gestures. There is a great difference between this naturalistic Corinthian epic style and the contemporary Attic refinement of narrative as seen in the François vase. Achilles, now a man, receives the armour, made by Hephaestus, from Thetis. But the couple is not now alone as in the Early Archaic version, for Thetis is accompanied by the Nereids and the whole incident of the meeting between mother and son has been made into a balladic scene of matchless happiness. It takes four women to carry the divine armour: Thetis herself brings the shield which has an emblem—designed to strike terror in the enemy—of unusual wildness and animation; three Nereids share the burden of the cuirass, greaves and helmet. The reverse of the vase shows the whole army of Myrmidons which Achilles commands. Although the painter may, himself, have been an Athenian, this manner of depicting a scene is Corinthian. We are familiar with the naturalistic style from the scene of the banquet of Eurytus and that of Peleus surprising Thetis.

Pls. 70b, c

Pl. 71a

Pls. 60a, III, 70b, c

We have another Corinthian example in the particularly delicately and carefully designed krater with a painting of Hector's farewell to his parents. The parting featured here is not the one from his wife Andromache which, in all its fateful depth, is well known to us from the *Iliad;* the scene shown here simply represents any departure as it may have taken place at the beginning of the war. Mounted troops, charioteers and infantry are all present; some

Pl. 71b

85

34 Achilles slaying Troilus. Shield-relief. Width of strip 5.2 cm. (2¹/₁₆ in.). c. 590–580 BC.—Olympia

35 Achilles slaying Troilus. Shield-relief. Width of strip 7.2 cm. (2¹³/₁₆ in.). c. 580 BC.—Olympia

of the inscribed names are very familiar from literary sources. Hector bids farewell to Priam and Hecabe. His charioteer is Cebriones who was a bastard of Priam and was later killed by Patroclus. Also present are the prophetess Cassandra and Priam's other daughter Polyxena who, after the conquest of Troy, was sacrificed on Achilles' tomb.

Pl. 72 The finest of these Corinthian kraters, however, is the one in the Astarita Collection which Beazley, with the help of a poem of Bacchylides, has been able to interpret. The illustrated episode takes place before the war has actually begun: Odysseus and Menelaus, led by the herald Talthybius, have come to Troy where they now sit on the steps of the city-wall. They have come to demand the return of Helen and to offer peace. In Troy the distinguished nobleman Antenor has always spoken in favour of a peaceful solution, so we can imagine him now on his way to Priam to tell the King of the arrival of the envoys. Meanwhile his wife Theano, priestess of Athene, comes, with many followers, to offer the guests greeting. The negotiations are unsuccessful, but the painter has made much of the episode. In spite of their splendid and gaily coloured clothes, the heroes do not give an impression of great confidence, whereas the women are seen as incomparably magnificent; this is especially true of Theano who is somewhat taller than her maidservants and has more abundant hair. She holds the spindle as do all women of princely houses in literature, even Artemis. Theano's white-haired nurse is also present. The only other occurrence of such a noble encounter of heroic women and foreign heroes is in the *Odyssey*, where Odysseus is welcomed to the Phaeacian court by the illustrious Arete.

> But then Odysseus
> threw his arms   round Arete's knees.
> The mist dispersed: they were all struck dumb,
> wondering at the man   and the manner of his coming.
> Odysseus besought her …
>
> *Odyssey* VII, 142–45

Pls. 46, 48a–c An incident of greater significance for the course of the action is Achilles' ambushing of Troilus, with which we are already familiar from the François vase, as it is the immediate cause of his own downfall. There is an amphora Pl. 73a which shows Achilles and Hector fighting over the body of Troilus at the foot of the altar; the latter is here given the form of the *omphalos* of Apollo at Delphi. Thus the painter indicates the wrath of the god, which Achilles

86

brings down on himself by committing murder within the sanctuary. This time, however, Achilles will prevail; he is, as usual, conducted by his loyal protectress Athene and by Hermes, whereas Hector's sole supporter is Aeneas.

One archaic feature of the legend of Troilus is preserved on a tripod-leg which dates from the beginning of the Figs. 28, 34 High Archaic period, as well as on early sixth-century shield-bands. Achilles has dragged the boy up over the altar; but the cock standing on the altar can only be interpreted as a love-gift. Kunze has seen in this, that a motif which had hitherto been taken as an invention of some Classical or Hellenistic poet can be traced even in the early period. According to the tradition, Achilles caught sight of Troilus as he lay in wait for him and fell in love with the boy; when Troilus refused to submit to him, Achilles killed him. This scene brings out an element of primitive savagery in Achilles which we will meet again, later, in the legend of Penthesilea but which remains hidden in Homer. Yet it is only this strange, pre-Homeric feature of the story which explains why the murder of a boy should have been represented at all as one of the acts of Achilles. In another relief, composed with even greater freedom and power, Troilus has taken refuge on the altar where, seeking protection, he embraces the sacred tree of Apollo. Fig. 35

The Early Archaic period provided only one type of scene characterizing the poem of the Wrath of Achilles:

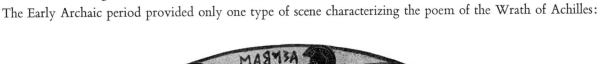

36 Duels between Ajax and Aeneas, and Achilles and Hector. Corinthian bowl from Dolon. *c.* 590–580 BC.—Brussels

Pls. 30, 31,
Fig. 28 this is the scene in which Hecabe goes, in supplication, to Athene. We now have, in addition, a second scene of supplication, in which the Achaeans visit Achilles. In this significant picture, which is still only of the late seventh century BC, the scene is depicted with a quiet dignity. As Achilles continues to stand aloof from the war, the Greeks find themselves in severe difficulties and so an attempt is made to make him change his mind (*Iliad* IX). Phoenix, whom we recognize by his herald's staff, walks in front. Odysseus who, as usual, is portrayed wearing a felt hat (*pilos*) follows, together with another warrior—probably Great Ajax; both of them shoulder spears, as distinct from Phoenix who has passed the age for military service. He has, instead, a crooked stick on which he carries the gift for Achilles suggested by the wise old man Nestor.

Fig. 36 The artist of one Corinthian bowl has represented two of the important battles from the poem of the Wrath of Achilles: these are the fight between Ajax and Aeneas over the body of Patroclus and the duel of Achilles and Hector. Ajax is backed by Little Ajax; this is frequently the case, but especially in the struggle for the body of Patroclus, in which Menelaus and Meriones rescue the dead warrior (*Iliad* XVII, 722ff.) whilst the two Ajaxes ward off the Trojans. The subject treated here is Achilles' greatest misfortune, *i.e.* the death of Patroclus, but on the other side of the bowl is the death of Hector (*Iliad* XXII, 248ff.). Achilles and Hector were certainly alone when they fought this duel, yet here we see Phoenix beside Achilles and Sarpedon beside Hector. In introducing these figures the artist is trying to say that the one was the last man to be really close to Achilles, whilst the other was the mightiest hero, next to Hector, on the Trojan side. Sarpedon had, in fact, fallen in the sixteenth book. These scenes do not actually reveal any very deep understanding of the original poem of the Wrath of Achilles, especially since, below one of the handles, the figure of Dolon appears. It has been positively proved that the book in which the incident with Dolon is described was not inserted in the *Iliad* until the 'Peisistratus edition,' and it is worth noting that the painter of this vase is already familiar with the 'Dolony' as a part of the *Iliad*. As the vase can scarcely be dated later than 570 BC, we must conclude that that version was made under Solon and that its influence quickly spread to Corinth.

Dolon was a Trojan spy who crept into the Greek camp by night. He was caught in the act by Odysseus and Diomedes who seized him and forced him to reveal the whereabouts of the camp of the Trojans' Thracian auxiliaries. Thus that same night Odysseus and Diomedes were able to surprise the sleeping Thracians who, under their king Rhesus, should, according to a prophecy, have brought the Trojans decisive aid.

Figs. 28, 36 So far the only scenes from the poem of the Wrath of Achilles which we have met are: the visit of supplication to Achilles, the struggle over the body of Patroclus and the death of Hector. Preference is, on the other hand, given to episodes which were added to the poem at a later time by the poet of the *Iliad*. Thus the *Aristia*, the book about the heroic deeds of Diomedes, is magnificently represented by the relief in which he is shown, with Athene as his Pl. 76a charioteer, driving at the savage War-god Ares. The figure of Athene is rather larger than that of the hero and the goddess is identifiable by the serpents on her aegis. The later poet's penchant for startling and impressive appearances and for miraculous signs finds correspondence in the way Diomedes brandishes his shield, and in the aegis bristling strangely about the goddess. Diomedes is not using his shield for defence, since he is protected by the goddess. In his new and daemonic greatness he realizes Athene's desire to do battle with Ares. Athene encourages her protégé to oppose even the gods in Ares and Aphrodite, and he succeeds in wounding both deities. Such an interplay of the divine and human spheres was alien to the poem of the Wrath of Achilles, yet now we immediately meet it Fig. 37 again in a second scene. Diomedes first fought with Aeneas. The fine painting on a tablet, of which, unfortunately, only half remains, is a representation of the duel between these two; it deviates from the poem in that we see Athene

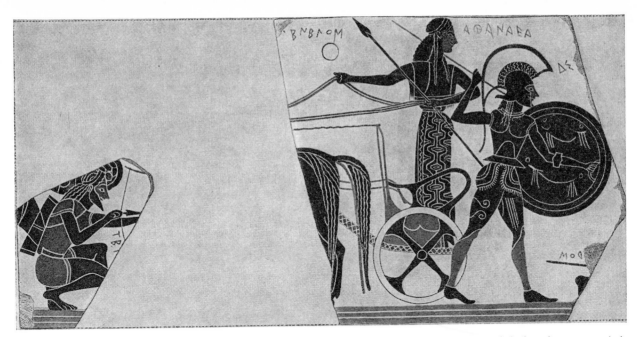

37 Corinthian votive tablet. On the right is Diomedes fighting Aeneas over Pandarus (only the . . . *ros* of the latter's name remains). The figure of Aeneas is missing. Athene is on Diomedes' chariot. On the left Teucrus kneels before Ajax. Height 8.3 cm. (3¹/₄ in.). *c.* 560 BC.—Berlin-Charlottenburg

already standing in the chariot whereas, in the *Iliad*, she does not mount it until later. The painter translates the poet's intentions into the language of visual art and thus shows how Athene is the constant support of the hero. In such pictures we sense the painter's feeling for and immediate understanding of these late parts of the *Iliad* as contemporary creations.

> She stepped into the chariot   and stood by Diomedes,
> eager for battle;   the heavy burden
> made the oak axle   creak under the weight
> of a mighty goddess   and a godlike man.
> Athene seized   the reins and whip,
> and steered the horses   straightway for Ares.
>
> *Iliad* V, 837–41

Representations of *Iliad* battles on Corinthian vases are less characteristic; artists take a general type of duel scene and add heroic names, as we have seen in connection with the bowl in Fig. 36. The poet of the *Iliad* created the scene in which the mighty Ajax fells Hector with a stone *(Iliad* XIV, 402 ff.), whereupon Aeneas and other Trojans come to Hector's help. The scene is illustrated by one Corinthian painter who has taken a commonly used Pl. 74 type of battle scene which he has provided with names from the *Iliad;* thereby having to take into the bargain the fact that Ajax now overpowers Hector with a spear instead of with a stone. This work, which belongs to the second quarter of the sixth century BC, also shows how remarkably strong, already at that time, was the influence of the poet of the *Iliad* on Corinthian art.

In the struggle over the body of Patroclus, Menelaus is opposed by a Trojan who must have been a more important figure than he is made to appear in the *Iliad*. The philosopher Pythagoras was convinced that his soul had
previously belonged to Euphorbus and, in the Sanctuary of Hera in Argos, Pausanias saw the shield which Menelaus
had stripped from Euphorbus in the battle. In the *Iliad* XVI, 806, Euphorbus inflicts the first wound on Patroclus.
In the following book he fights with Menelaus over the body, and falls himself. Hector and Menelaus now fight
Pl. 75 over Euphorbus; this scene is shown on an eastern Greek plate which is still only of the late seventh century BC.
The fact that the torso of the fallen warrior lies on the side of his opponent Menelaus is meant to indicate that
Menelaus is to receive Euphorbus' armour—otherwise he would not have been able to dedicate the shield in the
Argive Sanctuary of Hera. Yet, according to the poet of the *Iliad*, Menelaus does not receive the armour of Euphor-
bus. Our painter is thus following a tradition which is older than the *Iliad* as we know it.

In the *Iliad* XIX, 303 ff., the most distinguished Achaeans try to calm Achilles who is inconsolable at the death
of Patroclus. After his reconciliation with Agamemnon they hope to persuade him to take part in the war. On one
Pl. 73b Corinthian oinochoe the Achaeans are represented by Odysseus and the white-haired Phoenix. Athene also comes
to comfort Achilles and to invigorate him with nectar and ambrosia. On the oinochoe her place is taken by Thetis
who had already previously procured new armour from Hephaestus for Achilles. The painter of the Corinthian
oinochoe links together the motifs of the two goddesses' helping Achilles by showing Thetis, accompanied by two
Nereids, coming, as a comforter, to the bed of Achilles. The greaves and the shield from the wonderful armour
hang on the wall of the tent.

Fig. 36 Now Achilles leads the Greeks to new victories. He kills Hector in single combat, but the artists of this period
were less fascinated by this episode, which ended the old poem of the Wrath of Achilles, than by the close of the
Iliad by means of which the later poet brought the work to an expiatory conclusion. We first see the raging fury
of Achilles as he drags along behind him the body of his slain enemy, tied to his chariot. Then we have the funeral-
Pl. 51c rites and funeral-games in honour of Patroclus. These games we have already met on the François vase. A bowl by
Pl. VI Sophilus, which is roughly contemporary, shows the stand full of excited spectators. The painter is familiar with
their enthusiasm from the contests which used, at that time, to be held in the Panathenaea.

At the end of the *Iliad* the unhappy Priam, guided by Hermes, comes secretly by night to Achilles to beg from
him the body of Hector for burial. It is apparent that the master of one bronze relief was familiar with the great
Pl. 76b contemporary poem which he had 'deeply absorbed and fully translated into visual form' (Kunze). The fame of
this creation is attested by several formations of the same mould and also variants. It shows the lithe, active figure
of the god Hermes, the bowed father in his kingly robes; Achilles, full of vigorous youth, turning kindly towards
the supplicant and, on the ground, the heroic body of the dead Hector, protected against any disfigurement by
Aphrodite and Apollo; the composition formed by these extremely varied figures is an incomparably concentrated
unity, the dramatic power of which suggests that the work was produced *c.* 560 BC.

Fig. 38, Pl. 77 It is not until the High Archaic period that art is ripe for the portrayal of the encounter between Achilles and
Penthesilea. No man had yet been able to withstand the Amazon queen, a daughter of Ares, who had come to the
help of the Trojans after Hector's death. She inflicts heavy losses on the Greeks until she meets Achilles himself and
succumbs, conquered more by his daemonic appearance than by outer strength. Thus, at least, is how the episode
is depicted in shield-reliefs and, later, by Exekias and the Penthesilea painter. In the usual Archaic battle scene we
expect to find a balance, with the defeated party on the right-hand side of the picture. Penthesilea, however, 'falls
Fig. 38 back under the impact of the collision... The unusual orientation of the battle—from right to left—was no accidental

90

VI Funeral-games for Patroclus. Fragment of a mixing-bowl of Sophilus. Height of the fragment 5.2 cm. (2¹/₁₆ in.). c. 570–560 BC.—
Athens

38 Penthesilea being vanquished by Achilles. Shield-relief. Width of strip 7.2 cm. (2¹³/₁₆ in.). *c.* 600 BC.—Olympia

choice and neither was it retained by chance. For, whilst the defeated Penthesilea, who faces to the right, occupies the left-hand side of the picture, her figure receives the greater emphasis' (Kunze); we believe the later literary tradition in which her attacker is conquered by her beauty so that he grieves for her after he has slain her.

Pl. 76c, Fig. 14   Achilles must now fight Memnon and in this encounter he falls, struck by the arrow of Paris. Ajax, whose Pls. 49, 79 strength and courage make him second only to Achilles, rescues the fallen warrior from the battle. Thetis and the Nereids mourn Achilles in one of those pleasantly balladic Corinthian portrayals. Ajax does not receive Achilles' Pl. 32a armour even though he is the bravest of the Greeks. We already know the deeply affecting Early Archaic scene of Pl. 78a his lonely suicide. High Archaic artists depict the scene more richly; they think of the thread of events and of the consequences of these events for the Greeks. Odysseus and Diomedes are horrified to find Ajax dead after he has thrown himself on his sword. We see not only the monstrous deed but also its effect. We remember that Odysseus

39 The Wooden Horse. Corinthian aryballos. Height 13 cm. (5¹/₈ in.). *c.* 560 BC.—Paris

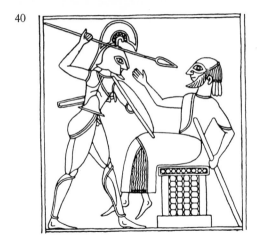

40   Death of Priam. Shield-relief. Width of strip 8.6 cm. (3³/₈ in.).
c. 570–560 BC.—Olympia

41   Death of Astyanax. Shield-relief. Width of strip 7.7 cm. (3 in.).
c. 580–570 BC.—Olympia

42   Ajax threatening Cassandra. Shield-relief. Width of strip 7.2 cm.
(2¹³/₁₆ in.). *c.* 590–580 BC.—Olympia

must bear responsibility for it. Yet he prefers to stand hidden behind his shield; Diomedes we recognize from his gesture of clutching at his neck.

The Sack of Troy is the subject of the painting on a Corinthian aryballos in which the artist has attempted to capture all the diverse activity about the Wooden Horse with something of a picture-book effect. We can recognize   Fig. 39 the armed attackers and the weaponless, surprised Trojans. In art of a higher level, individual scenes are selected. Neoptolemus, the son of Achilles, kills Priam despite the fact that the King had taken refuge on the altar of Zeus   Fig. 40 where he should be inviolable. The bald head of the aged, entreating man and the sceptre in his left hand make the sacrilege of the deed appear all the more dreadful. The sight of these evil deeds is meant to remind us of the anger of the gods and of all the disasters which, as a consequence, befall the Greeks on their journey home. A second outrage is the murder, by this same Neoptolemus, of Hector's little son Astyanax. In comparison with the Late   Fig. 41 Geometric conception of the scene, the version in the shield-relief is completely new. With a tremendous bound —made to appear all the greater by the foil of the huge, Boeotian shield—the warrior leaps at the boy, swinging him high into the air and threatening him with his raised sword. The unusual emptiness of the surface behind the boy could indicate that, as in the tale of Iliu Persis, he was flung from the city-wall.

Neoptolemus' two outrages, against Priam and Astyanax, are combined in a single scene by certain Attic painters, the first of whom is the C painter in his masterpiece, a pyxis with lid. The altar stands significantly in the centre,   Pl. 78b

93

43 Clytaemnestra and Aegisthus murdering Agamemnon. Shield-relief. Width of strip 7.2 cm. (2^{13}/$_{16}$ in.). *c.* 570–560 BC.—Olympia

44 Orestes murdering Aegisthus. Shield-relief. Width of strip 7.2 cm. (2^{13}/$_{16}$ in.). *c.* 580 BC.—Olympia

and the Gorgon on the shield beside it intensifies the atmosphere of horror. Later Attic versions of the scene show Priam taking refuge on the altar; with this feature the dramatic concentration of the action is finally complete, but the story as told in our painting still has epic variety and multiplicity. Priam and Hecabe stand to the left of the altar, lifting their hands in entreaty; they are more concerned about the fate of their grandson than about their own plight. Meanwhile the Greeks, both mounted and on foot, have broken into the city: there are three groups of seven, each group separated from the others by a horseman, which occupy all the rest of the frieze. Because the line is moving to the left, we are able to distinguish the various shield-emblems and this adds to the feeling of menace in the movement towards the left. It is because we read from left to right that the line of men seems to be coming towards us, so that we experience the horror of the happenings. Despite its epic richness, the narrative style of this painting comes close to the drama which characterizes Late Archaic art. The changed style corresponds completely to the dramatic quality in the actual idea of combining the outrages of Neoptolemus against Priam and Astyanax.

The name of Locrian Ajax was ill-famed on account of a third act of sacrilege. Intending to violate Cassandra, Fig. 42, Pl. 77 he tore her away from the image of Athene to which she was clinging for refuge. In many versions of this scene Cassandra's distress is especially brought out by her nakedness, whilst the sacrilege of Ajax's action is indicated by the presence of the altar. The frequency of these scenes of sacrilege is equalled by the repetition of their antithesis—to illustrate these we show the Spartan funerary stela rather than the shield-reliefs. Menelaus has drawn his sword as Pl. 69 he walks up to his regained wife; but Helen, confident of her effect, stands calmly before him.

We find the legend of the Heroes' Return represented by the same episodes that we have already met, but Fig. 43, Pl. 33 they are now shown with powerful concentration. In the scene of the murder of Agamemnon, Aegisthus holds the huge King down with a firm hand, whilst Clytaemnestra stabs him through the body from behind. In the epic, it is Aegisthus who is the murderer, Clytaemnestra merely acting as his assistant; at a later date both Pindar and Aeschylus take up that version of the legend which is shown in the relief. Pindar makes Clytaemnestra kill Agamemnon with a sword, whilst in Aeschylus she performs the deed with a hatchet, or double-axe. The King's dignity and his defenceless state are stressed, in the relief, by the spear placed to one side. The combination formed by the murderous lover and the false wife against the hero who, for the last time, desperately strives to turn the course of Pl. 76b Fate has a drama which recalls the similar composition in Priam's visit of supplication to Achilles, but it possesses even greater original power than this work and is even more typically High Archaic. The treacherous net is not used here and the figure of Aegisthus is given greater dignity than in later art. This is particularly true of the representation Fig. 44 of Orestes' revenge, which has even more of the typical High Archaic serenity and grandeur. Orestes, his spear

94

ready-aimed, rushes at the enthroned Aegisthus whom he grasps by the hair with his left hand. Aegisthus, bending forward as though preparing to leap to his feet, is drawing his sword from its scabbard. He is not shown as the despicable coward of later tradition, which may be linked with Early Archaic works. In these, Orestes' act represents the archetypal phenomenon of revenge and the hero himself is a daemonic figure; now, however, the deed is Pl. 36a understood as part of a sequence of events. His youth is characterized by his lack of beard. The magnificent throne is Agamemnon's and the traitor, having usurped it, is now overtaken by revenge.

A bronze relief from Olympia, in the Ionian style of Magna Graecia, shows a richer and less concentrated version of the murder of Clytaemnestra: with his left hand Orestes seizes her by the throat, thrusting his sword through Pl. 80 her body as she sinks back. On the right Aegisthus, looking round in horror, flees on to the steps of an altar; the woman unveiling herself on the left is Orestes' sister Electra, whose cooperation in the deed is otherwise known to us only from tragedy and from fifth-century representations of the episode.

We have what I should like to interpret as an important new illustration of part of the *Odyssey* on the splendid amphora from Melos. Hermes, sent by order of the Olympians, has to ask Calypso to release Odysseus; his zeal Fig. 45 and her friendly response conceal the pain which not even these divine beings are spared. This florid style, typical of the Ionian islands, is very well suited to the encounter on the paradisaic isle of Ogygia.

Hermes the messenger   marvelled as he stood.
But when he had gazed   in wonder at everything
he stepped inside   the spacious cave.
The fair Calypso   did not fail to recognize him,

45   Hermes visiting Calypso. Amphora from Melos. Height 1 m. (39³/₈ in.). *c.* 600 BC.—Athens

for the immortals always recognize   each other when they meet,
though one may dwell   in a distant home.

Most welcome guest,   God of the golden-wand,
it has not been your custom   to come to my home.
Say what you intend :   my spirit tells me
that I will fulfil it,   if fulfilled it may be.
But follow, I will provide   food and hospitality.

Odyssey V, 75–80, 87–91

If our interpretation is correct we are here seeing, for the first time, one of those scenes which are a precious legacy from the original *Odyssey*, in that their conception of the heroes is a Homeric one, based on inner experiences. There are no representations in later Classical art in which it can be said that Homer's conceptions of Odysseus and Calypso or of Nausicaa and the Phaeacians have really been made into pictorial images. It is not until the Classical period that we meet great representations of Odysseus and Eurycleia, Penelope, Telemachus and the killing of the suitors. In Archaic art, only the adventures with Polyphemus and the Sirens are represented, although Late Archaic artists also illustrate the adventure with Circe.

An Etruscan bucket from Chiusi, decorated with ivory reliefs, may go back to one of the Greek picture-books: on the left we see the ship of Odysseus with the helmsman who is being approached, from the right, by two of the companions. They are followed by four rams, a companion clinging to the belly of each one; the figure of Polyphemus in the entrance to his cave originally came next but the frieze is unfortunately damaged here. This all-inclusive type of epic narrative recalls the stylistic level of Clitias. We can also interpret the Late Corinthian aryballos in Boston on the basis of this style: we see Odysseus' ship as, with furled sails, it is rowed past the island of the Sirens by five warriors; the bow of the ship is in the shape of a boar's head and the poop projects high in the air. The helmeted figure of Odysseus stands tied to the mast and birds alight on the deck. To the right of the ship is the house of Circe, which Odysseus has just left, its door still wide-open. The mistress of the house sits sadly on the rock, gazing after Odysseus.

The works just discussed are mere illustrations; a finer work was a Late Corinthian krater of which only a small

Fig. 15, Pls. I, 16,
37, Fig. 46

Fig. 46

46 Odysseus and the Sirens. Corinthian aryballos. Height 10.2 cm. (4 in.). *c*. 560 BC.—Boston. (Circe's house, on the right in the illustration, should be imagined as being on the left of the ship on the actual vase)

96

fragment has survived. It shows the remains of a highly detailed portrayal of the escape of Odysseus from the cave of Polyphemus.

Illustrations of the *Odyssey* are less frequent than we might expect from the prevalence of elements of folklore in the legend. Many of the representations of the legend do not, moreover, have the character of vase-paintings, but are more like extracts from cheap picture-narratives, crammed with detail. The production of 'books' containing this type of scene-sequence corresponded to the popularity and the expansion of the legends among those strata of the population and those peoples who could not read. On the other hand, the vase-painters, the smiths who created the bronze reliefs and even the monumental artists picked out only those elements from the legend-sequences which were suitable mythological examples for use in the symposium or in the heroic atmosphere of the contests, or could be used on dedicatory gifts in sanctuaries. The dead could also be provided with such themes to accompany them, for their existence was imagined as a higher and more heroic one—nearer to the heroes of legend—than that of the living.

Homer in Archaic art

From the Homeric age until the epic renaissance in the sixth century BC there was a continuous increase in the number of representations of episodes from the various legend-cycles. In the end, poetry and the visual arts became unusually close to each other. The complete revival of narrative style at the time of Clitias was dependent, as we have seen, on the establishment of epic recitals, attested in the northern Peloponnese, and especially in Athens, from the High Archaic period onward. The themes are linked together by the motif of crime and punishment or by omens and the like. Artists are now trying to grasp the legends in all their diversity; in particular they attempt to individualize the circle of the Olympians and to make felt the tension between the divine and the human spheres.

Attic artists had the best conception of what constitutes the epic character. Corinthian art retains something of a down-to-earth ballad-like quality. Yet in a few isolated Corinthian works—such as the Amphiaraus krater and the   Pl. 67a
krater with the legation to Troy—there is some resemblance to the epic variety and combination of motifs charac-   Pl. 72
teristic of Attic art. In as far as the smallness of the format allows, the style of the Argive-Corinthian bronze reliefs
is determined by the spirit of epic narrative; this applies particularly to Priam's visit to Achilles and the departure   Pl. 76b
of Diomedes. Certainly we must not fail to appreciate the disparity between pictorial art and literature. The inde-   Pl. 76a
pendence of the former came out most clearly in the representation of the Sack of Troy by the C painter. There   Pl. 78b
are only a few, minor paintings, such as the Corinthian Wooden Horse, which seem a simple illustration.   Fig. 39

In general, pictorial art bears witness to the independent way in which the Greeks responded to the first great poet of the West. Homer's way of seeing things and his world—as created by his imagination—are the foundations, although artists constantly conceived and interpreted them anew. Thereby his successors remained creative artists as long as a genuine Greek character survived.

THE PLATES

Where a plate has more than one section the letters a–b–c indicate
a sequence from left to right and from top to bottom.

1 Harpist,
so-called Orpheus.
Marble statuette from
Amorgos in the
Cyclades. Later part
of third millennium BC

2 a. Attack on a sea-coast fortress. Silver relief on
a libation-vessel (rhyton) from Mycenae.—
b. Cult-scene. Gold seal-ring from Mycenae.—
Both *c.* 1500 BC

3 a. Female mourners, procession of warriors,
and warriors on war-chariots.—b. Departure of
warriors and return, by sea, from the campaign.—
Fragments of Attic Geometric kraters. Both before
750 BC

4 a. Zeus and Typhon (?). Bronze group from Olympia.—b. Apollo and Heracles struggling for the tripod (?). Leg of a bronze tripod from Olympia. *c.* 700 BC

5 a. Heracles fighting the lion (?). Clay tripod.—b. Heracles and the Stymphalian Birds (?). Oinochoe.—c. The abduction of Helen by Paris. Basin from Thebes.—All Late Geometric, second half of eighth century BC

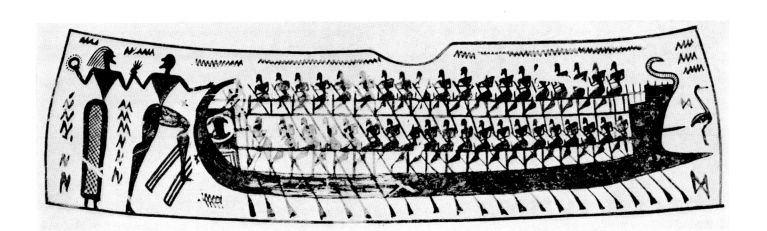

6 a. Heracles' fight with the Hydra, and the Wooden Horse. Bronze fibula from Thebes. Second half of eighth century BC.—b. Heracles and the Moliones. Bronze fibula from Crete. Later than 700 BC.—c. Nessus and Deianeira. Seal. *c.* 700 BC

7 a. Nestor and the sons of Actor. From an Attic, Late Geometric oinochoe. Second half of eighth century BC.—b. Heracles in battle with the Amazons. Clay shield from Tiryns. *c.* 700 BC

8 Shipwreck of Odysseus.
Attic, Late Geometric
oinochoe. 750–700 BC

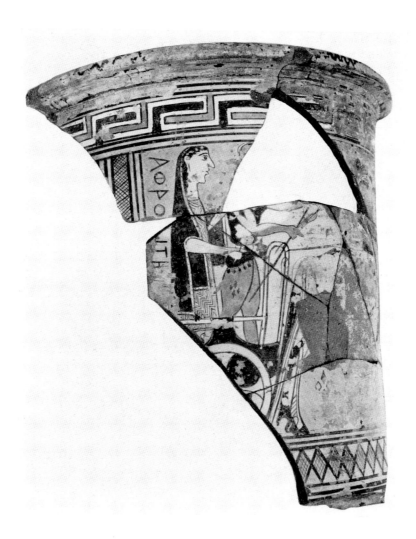

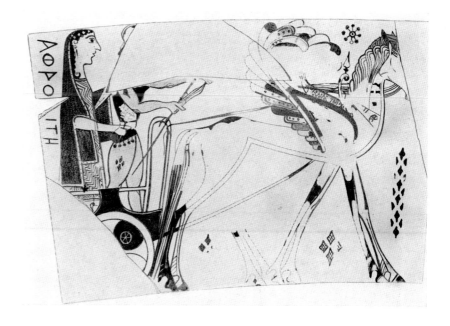

9 Aphrodite and Ares driving a chariot.
From the neck of an amphora from Naxos.
c. 660 BC. Original and copy

10 Apollo meeting Arte-
mis. Amphora from Melos.
On the neck: Achilles and
Memnon in single combat.
c. 650 BC

11 a. Punishment of Prometheus. Ivory relief from Sparta.—b. Europa on the bull. From a relief-decorated
amphora.—Both *c.* 650 BC

12 Leto giving birth to Apollo (?). From a relief-decorated amphora from Thebes. Post 700 BC

13 Birth of Athene (?). From a relief-decorated amphora from Tenos. First half of seventh century BC

14 Two goddesses.
Ivory group. *c.* 660 BC

16 The Gorgons pursuing Perseus. Early Attic amphora from Eleusis. On the neck: Odysseus blinding Polyphemus. *c.* 670 BC. Cf. Plate I

17 Perseus slaying the Gorgon. Ivory relief from Samos. *c.* 630–620 BC

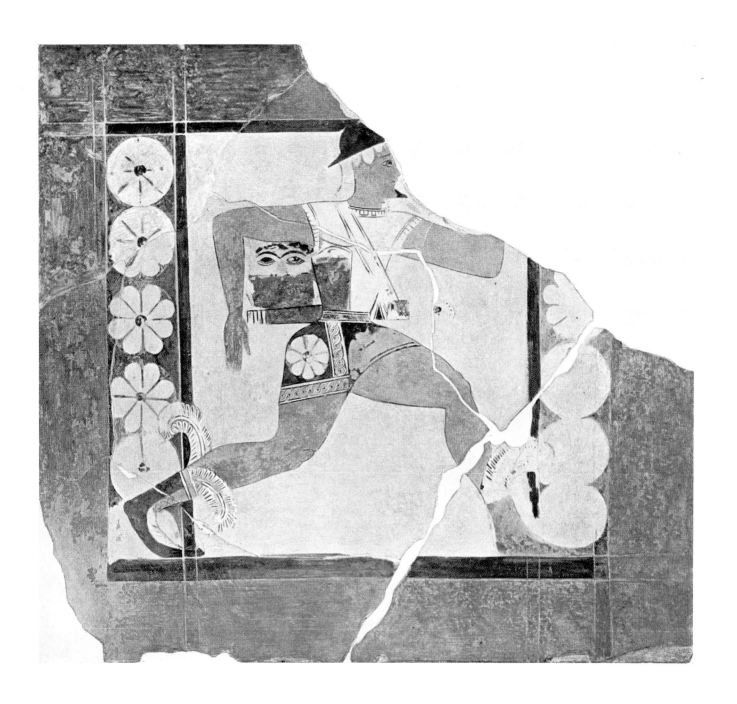

18   Perseus fleeing from the Gorgons. Clay metope from the Temple of Apollo in Thermos. *c.* 625 BC

20   Chelidon and Aëdon. Clay metope from the Temple of Apollo in Thermos. *c.* 625 BC

21 Orion (?). Clay metope from the Temple of Apollo in Thermos. *c.* 625 BC

22 Bellerophon and the Chimaera. Fragment of a Protocorinthian scyphus. *c.* 670 BC

23 Heracles slaying the Centaur Nessus. Early Attic amphora. *c.* 680 BC

24 a. Heracles chasing the Centaurs.
Protocorinthian lekythos. *c.* 660 BC.—
b. Heracles slaying the Centaur Nessus.
Ivory relief from Sparta. *c.* 670–660 BC.—
c. Thetis giving Achilles his weapons. From
a Cycladic neck-amphora from Delos.
c. 670 BC

25 a. The children of Athens fighting
against the Minotaur. From a relief-
decorated amphora. *c.* 670–660 BC.—
b. Achilles and the cattle of Aeneus. From
a relief-decorated amphora from Thebes.
c. 650 BC

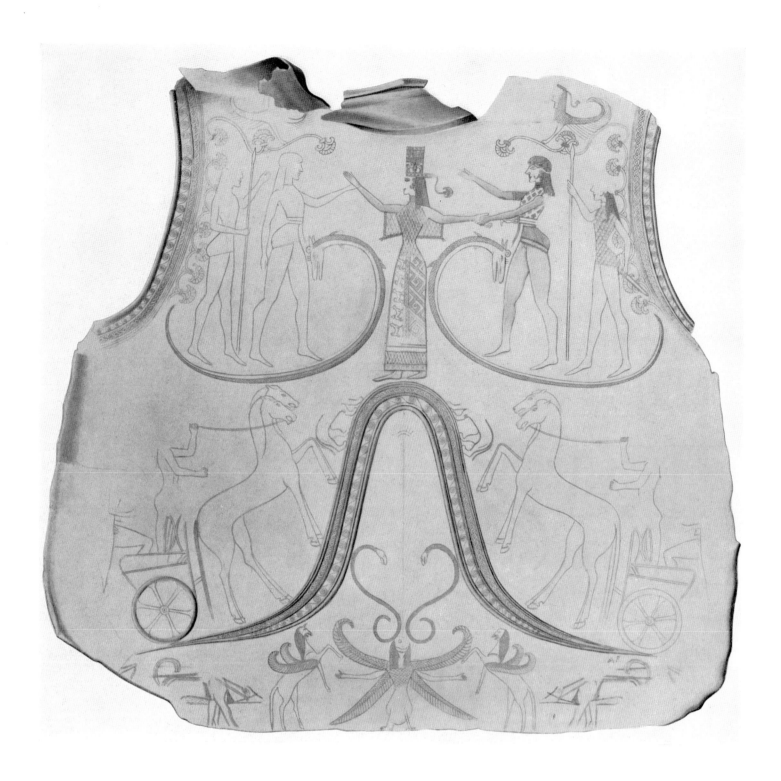

26   The Dioscuri rescuing Helen from Theseus and Perithous. Bronze cuirass from Olympia. *c.* 670–660 BC

27 a, b. Theseus wooing Ariadne. a. Clay relief from Tarentum. b. From a Cretan oinochoe from Arcadia. Both early part of seventh century BC.—c. Caeneus and the Centaurs. Bronze relief from Olympia. *c.* 630 BC

28 Peleus and Thetis. Clay relief from Tegea. *c.* 650 BC

29 a. Peleus consigning the child Achilles to the Centaur Cheiron. From an Early Attic amphora. *c.* 680 BC.—b. Judgment of Paris. From the so-called Chigi Vase. *c.* 640–630 BC.—c. Chariot-ride of Patroclus. Protocorinthian aryballos. *c.* 630 BC

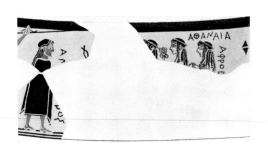

30, 31 Hecabe and her maid-servants
going to Athena with the robe-offering.
From a relief-decorated amphora. *c.* 660 BC

32   a. Suicide of Ajax. Seal from Peraea, Corinth.—b. Ajax with body of Achilles. Fragment of a clay relief, from Tarentum?—c. Clytaemnestra murdering Cassandra. Bronze plate from the Heraeon of Argos.—All datable to first half of seventh century BC

33 Murder of Agamemnon. Clay relief from Gortyna. Second quarter of seventh century BC

34 Scenes depicting the conquest of Troy. Relief-decorated amphora from Mykonos. On the neck: the Trojan Horse. *c.* 670 BC

35 a. The Trojan Horse.—b. Menelaus threatening Helen.—From the neck and shoulder respectively of the relief-decorated amphora from Mykonos. Cf. Plate 34

36 a. Orestes slaying Aegisthus. From an Early Attic krater. *c.* 680–670 BC.—b. Death of Aegisthus. From a relief-decorated amphora from Thebes. Second quarter of seventh century BC

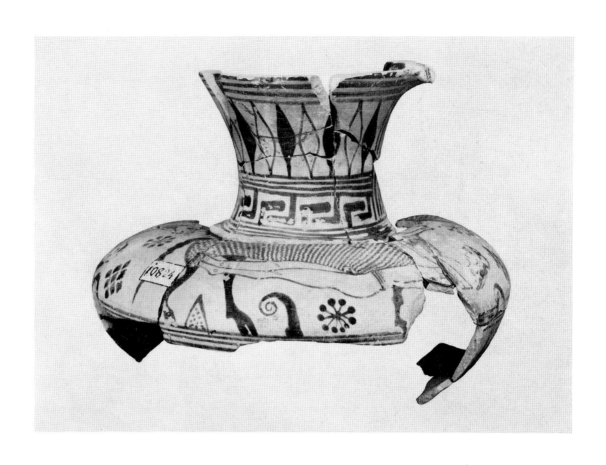

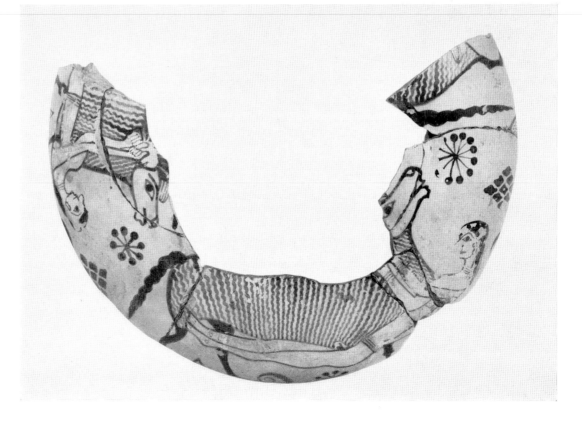

37 Escape from the cave of Polyphemus. Fragments of an Early Attic oinochoe from Aegina. *c*. 660 BC

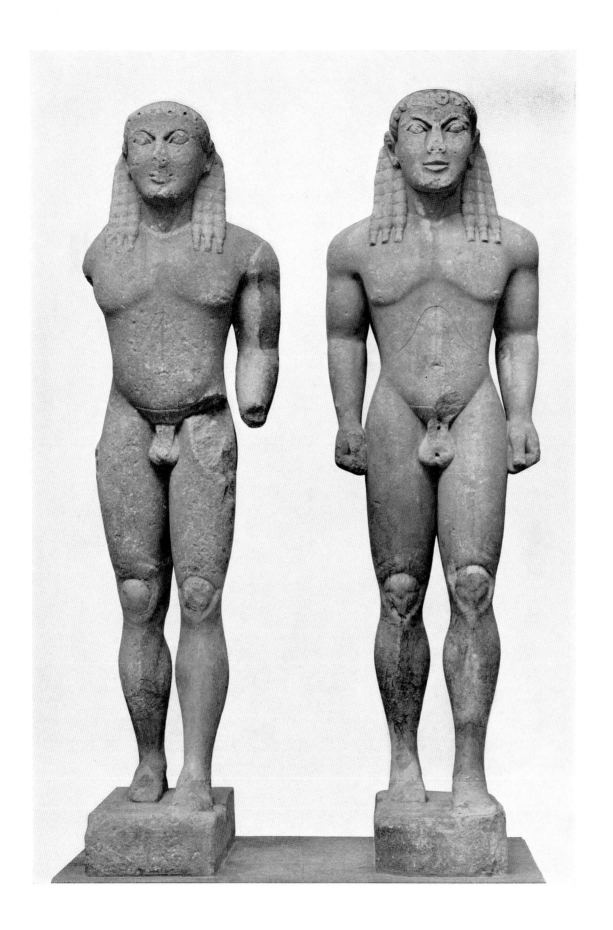

38 Cleobis and
Biton.
Marble statues.
Post-600 BC

39 The holy marriage of
Zeus and Hera. Wooden
relief from the Heraeon on
Samos. *c.* 620 BC

40   a. Aristaeus. From an Early Attic oinochoe of the Ceramicus Painter. *c.* 600 BC.—b. Bellerophon and the Chimaera. From an Early Attic krater of the Chimaera Painter. *c.* 610 BC

41 a. Punishment of Prometheus. Shield–relief. *c.* 590 BC.—b. Zeus, accompanied by Nike and a serpent, wielding his thunderbolt against the Titans (?). Fragment of a column–krater of Lydos. *c.* 560 BC

42 Cronus or Rhea.
From the west gable of the
Temple of Artemis on Corfu.
c. 590 BC

43 Zeus and a Titan
(Iapetus?).
From the west gable
of the Temple of
Artemis on Corfu.
c. 590 BC

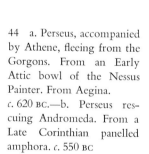

44   a. Perseus, accompanied by Athene, fleeing from the Gorgons. From an Early Attic bowl of the Nessus Painter. From Aegina. *c.* 620 BC.—b. Perseus rescuing Andromeda. From a Late Corinthian panelled amphora. *c.* 550 BC

45   Perseus fleeing from the Gorgons. Mixing-bowl of the Gorgon Painter. Post-600 BC

46   Volute-krater of Clitias. Front view. *c.* 570 BC. Cf. Plates 47–52

47   Hunt of the Calydonian Boar. From the volute-krater of Clitias. Cf. Plate 46

50   Volute-krater of Clitias. Rear view. *c.* 570 BC. Cf. Plates 46–52

51   From the volute-krater of Clitias. a and b. Arrival on Delos of the children of Athens; Lapiths and Centaurs.
Cf. Plate 50.—c. Funeral-games for Patroclus. Cf. Plate 46

52   The return of Hephaestus to Olympus. From the volute-krater of Clitias. Cf. Plate 50

53   Apollo and Artemis slaying the children of Niobe. From a Tyrrhenian amphora. *c.* 565 BC

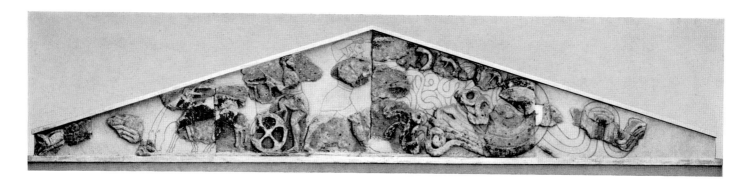

54 a. Heracles and the Hydra. Limestone gable from the Acropolis in Athens. *c.* 590 BC.—b. Apollo slaying Tityus. From a neck-amphora of the painter of Vatican 309. *c.* 565 BC.—c. Heracles slaying the Hydra. Corinthian skyphos. *c.* 580 BC

55 a. Heracles wrestling with Nereus. Fragment of a hydria of the Comast Group. *c.* 580 BC.—b. Europa on the bull. Metope from the Treasury of Sicyon. *c.* 570 BC

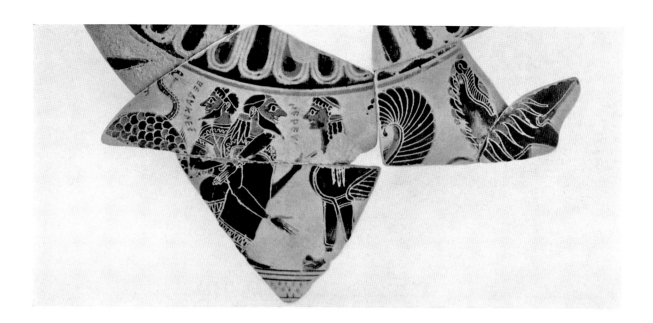

56   a. Heracles wrestling with Triton.—b. Triple-bodied being (Nereus?).
From the gable of the ancient Temple of Athena on the Acropolis in Athens. Limestone. *c.* 570 BC

57a.　Heracles rescuing Prometheus. From an Early Attic krater of the Nessus Painter. From Vari. *c.* 610 BC.—b. Paris abducting Helen; Heracles slaying Geras. Shield–relief from Olympia. *c.* 500 BC.—c. Heracles and Deianeira taking leave of Deianeira's parents. From an amphora from Melos. *c.* 600 BC

58 a. Heracles slaying Andromache in the battle with the Amazons. From a neck-amphora of the Camtar Painter. *c.* 560 BC. —b. Theseus slaying the Minotaur; Heracles wrestling with Achelous. From a Corinthian bowl. *c.* 690 BC.—c. Death of Astyanax. From a lekythos from Gela. *c.* 560 BC

59 The Gorgons pursuing Perseus. Amphora of the Nessus Painter. On the neck: Heracles slaying Nessus. *c.* 610 BC

ΒΥΡΥΓΕΟΜ
ΜΟΤΖΦΘΞ·
ΛΕΟΓΑ
ΕΒΡΑΧΛΘΒΒ

ΑΤΑΛΑΝΤΑ

60   a. Heracles catching sight of Iole at the banquet of Eurytus. From a Corinthian krater. *c.* 600 BC. Cf. Plate III.—b. Atalanta in the Calydonian boarhunt. Fragment of a mixing-bowl. *c.* 570 BC

61 a. Heracles and the Cercopes. Shield-relief. *c.* 560 BC.
—b. The Calydonian boar
and its victim, Ancaeus.
Fragment of a mixing-bowl.
c. 570 BC

62 Heracles and the Centaurs from the mountains of Pholoë. Corinthian scyphus. Front and reverse. *c.* 580 BC

63 a. The Argo with
Orpheus, the Dioscuri
and Argonauts.—b. The
Dioscuri and the Aphare-
tids (Idas and Lycneus)
carrying off a herd of
cattle. Metope from the
Treasury of Sicyon.
c. 570 BC

64 a. Harpies. From a bowl from Aegina. *c.* 620 BC.—b. Uninterpreted scene, Boreads and Harpies. From an ivory relief. *c.* 570 BC

65 Funeral-games for Pelias. Three fragments of a mixing-bowl. *c.* 580–570 BC

66   Zeus and Typhon. Chalcidian hydria. Reverse. *c.* 550 BC

67   a. The departure of Amphiaraus. From a Corinthian krater.—b. Judgment of Paris. Tyrrhenian amphora of Lydes.—Both *c.* 560 BC

68, 69 Menelaus
wooing Helen.—
Menelaus threat-
ening Helen. Grave-
stelae from Sparta.
c. 580–570 BC

70   a. Wedding of Paris and Helen. From a Corinthian krater. *c.* 580 BC.—b, c. Peleus surprising Thetis and the Nereids.
From a Corinthian krater. *c.* 560 BC

71   a. Thetis, accompanied by the Nereids, handing Achilles his weapons. From an amphora of the Camtar Painter.—b. Hector setting out to battle. From a Corinthian krater.—Both *c.* 570–560 BC

72 The Greek ambassadors in Troy being greeted by Theano. Corinthian krater. *c.* 570–560 BC

73 a. Hector and Achilles fighting over Troilus. Tyrrhenian amphora. *c.* 570–560 BC.— b. Thetis comforting her son Achilles. From a Corinthian oinochoe. *c.* 570 BC

74   Hector and Ajax in combat.
Corinthian oinochoe. *c.* 570 BC

75   Menelaus and Hector fighting over the fallen Euphorbus. 'Cnidian' plate. *c.* 610 BC

76 a. Athene on Diomedes'
chariot. Bronze relief from
Olympia. *c.* 570 BC.—
b. Priam begging Achilles
for the body of Hector.
Bronze handle-plaque from
a hand-mirror. *c.* 560 BC.—
c. Achilles and Memnon in
single combat. *c.* 580 BC

77 Left: birth of Athene;
Achilles and Penthesilea.
Right: Ajax and Cassandra;
Heracles and Geryon.
Shield-relief strip from
Delphi. *c.* 560 BC

78 a. Odysseus and Diomedes finding Ajax, who has thrown himself on his sword. Scene on the reverse of the krater in Plate III. *c.* 600 BC.—b. Death of Astyanax. From the lid of a pyxis from Cumae. *c.* 570–560 BC

79 Achilles being mourned by the Nereids. Corinthian hydria. *c.* 570 BC

80 Centre: Orestes slaying Clytaemnestra. Below: Theseus winning the Amazon Antiope. Bronze relief from Olympia. *c.* 570 BC

ACKNOWLEDGEMENTS

Since the discovery and publication of the pithos from Mykonos, which we owe to Miriam Ervin, we are able to see even more clearly than before that the cyclic epics form the final stage of a diverse literary tradition of story-telling. This final stage applies only to the later illustrations in this volume, *i.e.* to the sixth century. The pithos has taught us to see the earlier illustrations in a new light as evidence of a type of legend-narration which is not yet canonical. Now we can also understand better why, in the early part of the sixth century, there could be such a barbaric conception of Achilles' murder of Troilus: the artist had not yet met the gentler representation in the cyclic epic of the *Cypria*.

After a few introductory plates the rest of the illustrations are arranged in three sections: the Homeric period; the period of the early lyric; the High Archaic period. Within these sections, where spacing has not forced us to alter the arrangement, we find, in the first place, illustrations of legends about the gods, then Bellerophon, Perseus, Heracles, Theseus, the Argonauts and the Theban and Trojan legends. Individual illustrations are enlarged as the effect is much more powerful than if the original size of the photographs is retained. Wherever possible, however, the dimensions are given with the bibliographical notes, so there can be no doubt about the original proportions.

For the reproduction material in the text I have to thank, in particular, Emil Kunze and his Institute in Athens; for forty years he has rendered the greatest service to the worthwhile reproduction of archaic art.

For individual material I must also thank Pierre Amandry, Ernst Berger, Rolf Blatter, Dietrich von Bothmer, Giacomo Caputo, Pierre Devambez, Hans Diepolder, José Dörig, Adolf Greifenhagen, Christos Karusos, Nikolaos Kontoleon, Doro Levi, Dieter Ohly, Cornelius Vermeule and Nikolaos Yaluris: I hope that they may find pleasure in the fine reproductions of the entrusted treasures and that they will accept in a friendly spirit this attempt to see them in a new connection. Finally my thanks go to Max Hirmer and his co-workers for their indefatigable care in the production of this book.

The design for Plate 26 was produced by the draughtsman Alex. Papailiopulos, under the direction of Nikolaos Yaluris, in months of work, from the scarcely decipherable engraving on the cuirass. The detailed publication is reserved for its discoverer, Nikolaos Yaluris.

Photographic sources: Athens, Agora Excavations: 7a. – Athens, Deutsches Archäologisches Institut: 1, 3a/b, 4b, 5a, 6b, 7b, 9, 11a, 12, 13, 17, 19–22, 24b/c, 27c, 28, 32c, 34, 35a/b, 37, 39–43, 55a/b, 57a–c, 61a, 64b, 65, 68, 69, 76a, 80. – Basle, Archäologisches Museum: 25a. – Basle, Archives D. Widmer: 29b. – Berlin, Staatliche Museen, Antikensammlung: 24a, 44b, 76c. – Berlin-Charlottenburg, Staatliche Museen, Antikenabteilung: 29a, 36a, 44a, 64a, 76b. – Boston, Museum of Fine Arts: 25b, 30, 31, 36b, 71a. – Brussels, Musée du Cinquantenaire: 73b. – Cambridge, England, Sir J. D. Beazley: 72. – Cambridge, England, Fitzwilliam Museum: 58a. – Florence, Alinari: 55b, 74. – Florence, Soprintendenza alle Antichità: 67b. – Hamburg, Museum für Kunst und Gewerbe: 53. – Heraklion, Museum: 15a, 33.– London, British Museum: 6a. – Munich, Hirmer Verlag, Archives: 2a/b, 6c, 10, 16, 38, 45–52, 56a/b, 59, 60a, 63a/b, 66, 73a, 75, and Colour Plates I–VI. – Munich, Staatliche Antikensammlungen, Museum Antiker Kleinkunst: 8. – Naples, Soprintendenza alle Antichità: 32b. – New York, Metropolitan Museum of Art: 4a, 14, 23, 32a, 70a. – Olympia, Museum: 26. – Paris, Archives M. Chuzeville: 15b, 54c, 62, 70b/c, 71b, 78a, 79. – Taranto, Soprintendenza alle Antichità: 27a. – Zurich, Prof. Dr. Bloesch: 60b, 61b.

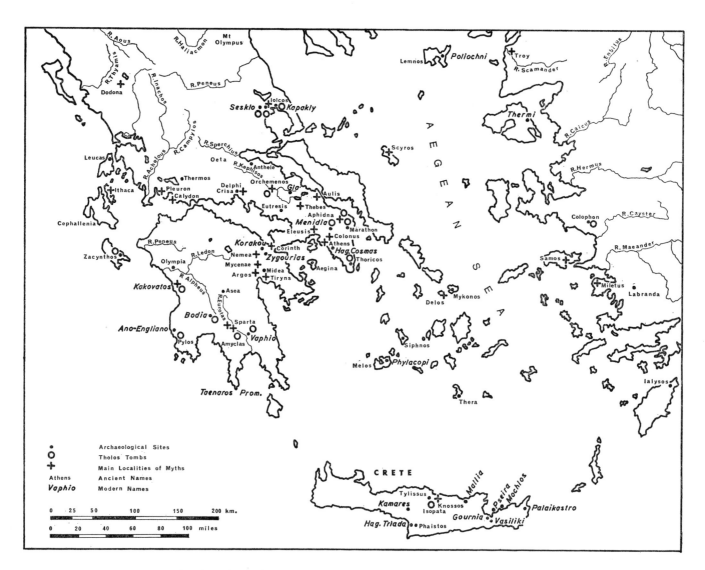

Archaeological sites, homes of the legends, their scenes of action and their heroes

Pylos	Sparta	Argos	Mycenae	Tiryns	Corinth	Aegina	Athens	Thebes	Thessaly	Crete	The West
	Hyacinthus	Pelops				Aeacus	Cecrops	Cadmus			Oenomaus
			Perseus		Bellerophon			Laius			
				Heracles		Telamon	Theseus	Oedipus	Jason	Minos	Meleager
								Antigone			Tydeus
		Adrastus	Atreus								
Nestor	Menelaus		Agamemnon			Ajax			Achilles	Idomeneus	Odysseus
						(Salamis)					Diomedes

182

I

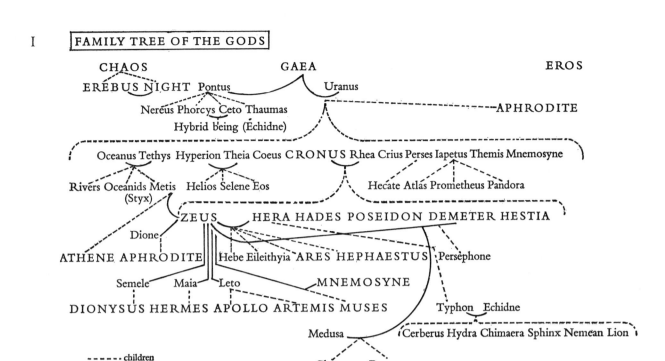

II FAMILY OF AEOLUS   The Diffusion of the Greeks

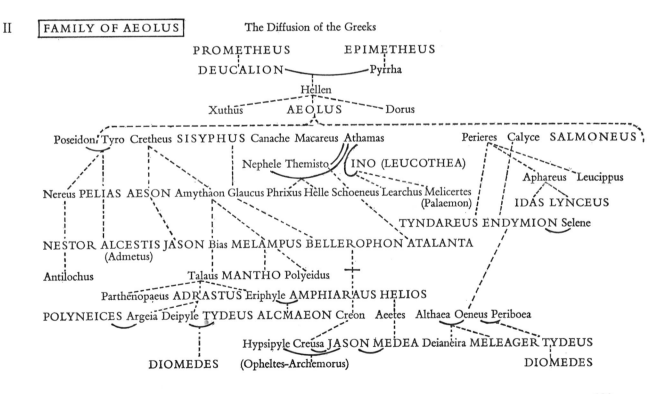

┌─────────────────────┐
FAMILY OF INACHUS The influence of the East

INACHUS

IO ZEUS

Epaphus

Libya Poseidon

Agenor Belus Anchinoë

Zeus EUROPA Phoenix Cilix CADMUS Harmonia AEGYPTUS DANAUS

Pasiphaë Minos Rhadamanthus Ino SEMELE Polydorus Autonoë Agave Echion Lynceus Hypermnestra Amymone

Aristaeus

Minotaur Ariadne Deucalion Glaucus Menoeceus Labdacus Actaeon Pentheus Abas (of Argos)

(Daedalus) Idomeneus (Polyeidus) Creon Iocaste Laius

(Icarus)

Megara Haemon OEDIPUS

Eteocles Polyneices ANTIGONE Ismene TANTALUS

Zeus Antiope

NIOBE Amphion Zethus → Dirce

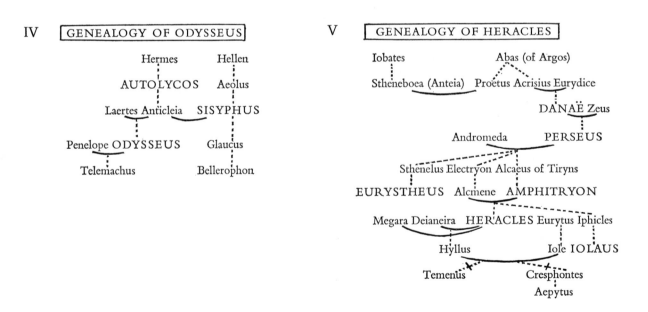

IV ┌─────────────────────────┐
GENEALOGY OF ODYSSEUS

V ┌─────────────────────────┐
GENEALOGY OF HERACLES

Hermes Hellen

AUTOLYCOS Aeolus

Laertes Anticleia SISYPHUS

Penelope ODYSSEUS Glaucus

Telemachus Bellerophon

Iobates Abas (of Argos)

Stheneboea (Anteia) Proetus Acrisius Eurydice

DANAË Zeus

Andromeda PERSEUS

Sthenelus Electryon Alcaeus of Tiryns

EURYSTHEUS Alcmene AMPHITRYON

Megara Deianeira HERACLES Eurytus Iphicles

Hyllus Iole IOLAUS

Temenus Cresphontes

Aepytus

VI THE TROJAN ROYAL FAMILY

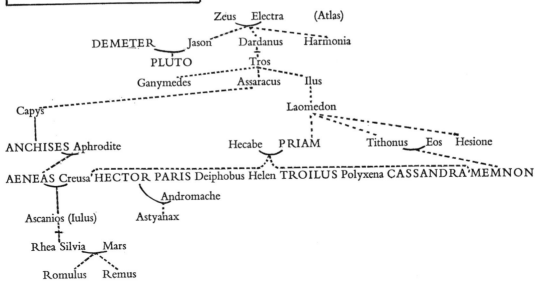

VII GENEALOGY OF AJAX AND ACHILLES

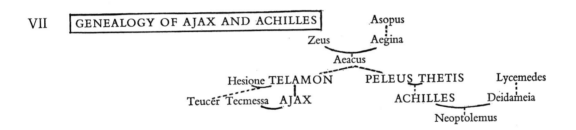

VIII THE TANTALIDS (MYCENAE)

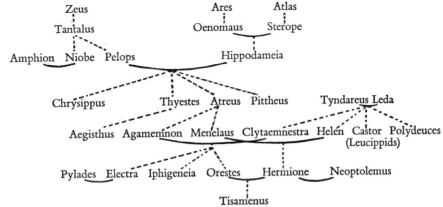

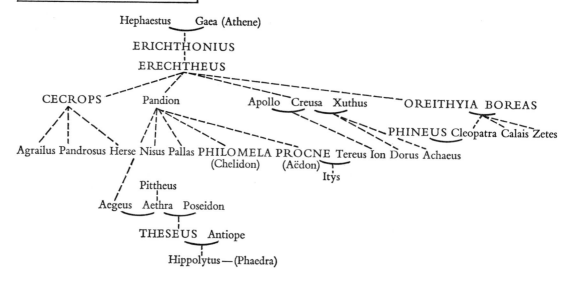

IX GENEALOGY OF THESEUS

Hephaestus   Gaea (Athene)

ERICHTHONIUS

ERECHTHEUS

CECROPS   Pandion   Apollo Creusa Xuthus   OREITHYIA BOREAS

PHINEUS Cleopatra Calais Zetes

Agrailus Pandrosus Herse Nisus Pallas PHILOMELA PROCNE Tereus Ion Dorus Achaeus
(Chelidon)   (Aëdon)

Itys

Pittheus

Aegeus Aethra Poseidon

THESEUS Antiope

Hippolytus — (Phaedra)

CHRONOLOGICAL TABLE

2000–1700 BC First flowering of Cretan civilization

1700–1400 BC Second flowering of Cretan civilization

1600–1200 BC Flowering of Mycenaean civilization

1000– 900 BC Protogeometric style, beginning of Greek art in its narrower style

 900– 700 BC Geometric style, indefinite tectonics

 700– 625 BC Early Archaic style, tectonics of surface only

 625– 560 BC High Archaic style, tectonics of volume

 560– 500 BC Late Archaic style, tectonics with elastic arrangement of elements

 500– 325 BC Classical style

 325– 100 BC Hellenistic style

186

NOTES

In my interpretation of the history of the archaic epic I have followed: 1. Erich Bethe, *Homer* (cf. in particular the review of literature and the evidence for the epic cycle in Vol. 2, 1922 (1929), 149 ff.); 2. Peter Von der Mühll, *Die Dichter der Odyssee*, in 68th *Jahresb. d. Ver. Schweiz. Gymnasiallehrer* (Aarau 1940); also the article in *Realencycl. der Klass. Altertumswiss.*, 7th Supplement (1940), 696 ff., and his *Kritisches Hypomnema zur Ilias*, 1952. The remarks on p. 8 ff. of the last-mentioned work, on the subject of the editing of the epics in the sixth century, are worth noting ('Peisistratos').

In *Die Quellen der Ilias*, 1960, W. Kullmann has attempted to date the epic cycle before the *Iliad*. The sequence I have suggested here seems to explain the observations which led him to this conclusion in a way more appropriate to the development of style in the visual arts; in particular I can apply what he says about the style of the cycle only to the sixth century (cf. also F. Jonan, *Rev. des Et. Gr.* 1961, 484 ff.). Kullmann's basic premise is that the *Iliad*, to a large extent, bears witness to the existence of the material of the cyclical epics but has left no clear traces in these epics. Could not the explanation lie in Friis Johansen's observation (see below) that it was not until the later sixth century that artists began to show a preference for the *Iliad* over the cyclical epics and to gain a deeper understanding of it?

I have given further references in *Museum Helveticum* 12, 1955, 132 ff., and 19, 1962, 130 ff. On the question of the dating of the cycle the remarks of E. Bethe, *loc. cit.* 2, 339 ff. and 3, 162 ff., are still standard. If, in his *Götterbeistand*, G. Beckel had made sharper historical divisions, it would have been clear from the interesting problems he presents and the illustrations he has assembled that the presence of the gods originally belonged only to the depiction of less extraordinary experiences (the Wrath of Achilles or the Deeds of Perseus), whereas, at the time of the epic renaissance from 600, it was looked for wherever remotely possible. Cf. I. Inckers, *Rev. Gnomon* 1963, 634 ff.

For any further pursuit of the archaeological side of the subject the following works are probably the most important (Kunze's book is a veritable manual of archaic illustrations of legend):

H. Luckenbach, 'Das Verhältnis der griechischen Sagenbilder zu den Gedichten des epischen Kyklos,' 11th suppl. to *Fleckeisens Jahrbücher f. class. Philol.* 1880, 491 ff.

W. H. Roscher, *Ausf. Lexikon der griechischen und römischen Mythologie*, Leipzig 1884

A. Schneider, *Der troische Sagenkreis in der ältesten griechischen Kunst*, 1886

C. Robert, *Bild und Lied*, Berlin 1891

L. Preller, *Griechische Mythologie*, 4th ed. edited by Carl Robert, Berlin 1894

F. Müller, *Die antiken Odysseeillustrationen*, Berlin 1913

C. Robert, *Arch. Hermeneutik*, Berlin 1919

E. Bethe, *Homer 2*, 1922, 149 ff.

K. Bulas, *Eos 34*, 1923/4, 241 ff.

K. Bulas, *Les illustrations antiques de l'Iliade*, Lemberg 1929

H. Payne, *Necrocorinthia*, A Study of Corinthian Art in the Archaic Period, Oxford 1931

K. Friis Johansen, *Iliaden i tidlig graesk kunst*, Copenhagen 1934

R. Hampe, *Frühe griechische Sagenbilder*, Athens 1936

P. Von der Mühll, *Die Dichter der Odyssee*, Aarau 1940

E. Kunze, *Archaische Schildbänder*, Berlin 1950

J. D. Beazley, *Development of Attic Black-Figure*, London 1951

K. Kerényi, *Griechische Mythologie*, Zurich 1951

R. Hampe, *Gleichnisse Homers*, Tubingen 1952

P. Von der Mühll, *Hypomnema zur Ilias*, Basle 1952

F. Brommer, *Herakles*, 1953

H. J. Rose, *A Handbook of Greek Mythology*, 5th ed. London 1953

K. Schefold, 'Archäologisches zum Stil Homers,' *Mus. Helv.* 12, 1955, 132 ff.

J. D. Beazley, *Attic Black-Figure Vase-Painters*, Oxford 1956

J. Schäfer, *Studien zu den griechischen Reliefpithoi*, 1957

T. J. Dunbabin, *The Greeks and Their Eastern Neighbours*, London 1957

K. Kerényi, *The Heroes of the Greeks*, London 1959

K. Schefold, *Griechische Kunst als religiöses Phänomen*, 1959

H. Hunger, *Lexikon der griechischen und römischen Mythologie*, 5th ed. 1959

M. R. Scherer, *The Legends of Troy in Art and Literature*, New York – London 1963

A. Heubeck, 'Zur neueren Homerforschung' (Literaturbericht), *Gymnasium 71*, 1964, 43–72

ABBREVIATIONS

Ant. Denkm.	*Antike Denkmäler*, Berlin 1831–1926
Beazley	J. D. Beazley, *Attic Black-Figure Vase-Painters* (1956)
Beazley D.	J. D. Beazley, *The Development of Attic Black-Figure* (1951)
Bibl. Nat.	Paris, Bibliothèque Nationale
Brommer	Frank Brommer, *Vasenlisten zur griechischen Heldensage*, 2nd ed. (1960)
CVA	Corpus Vasorum Antiquorum
Dunbabin	T. J. Dunbabin, *The Greeks and Their Eastern Neighbours* (1957)
GGA	Göttinger Gelehrte Anzeigen
HdA	Handbuch der Archäologie
Hampe	Roland Hampe, *Frühe griechische Sagenbilder in Böotien* (1936)
Hampe G.	Roland Hampe, *Die Gleichnisse Homers und die Bildkunst seiner Zeit* (1952)
Kunze	Emil Kunze, 'Archaische Schildbänder,' *Olympische Forschungen* II (1950)
Lippold	Georg Lippold, *Die griechische Plastik*. HdA 3 (1950)
Matz	Friedrich Matz, *Geschichte der griechischen Kunst* I. *Die Geometrische und die früharchaische Form* (1950)
Metr. Mus.	New York, Metropolitan Museum
Mus. Helv.	Museum Helveticum
NM	Nationalmuseum
Payne	Humphry Payne, *Necrocorinthia*, A Study of Corinthian Art in the Archaic Period (1931)
Riccioni	G. Riccioni, 'Origine e sviluppo del Gorgoneion,' *Rivista dell'Istituto di Archeologia* 18, 1960, 127–206
Rumpf	A. Rumpf, *Malerei und Zeichnung*. HdA 4 (1953)
Schäfer	Jürg Schäfer, *Studien zu den griechischen Reliefpithoi des 8.–6. Jh. v. Chr. aus Kreta, Rhodos, Tenos und Boiotien* (1957)

ILLUSTRATIONS WITHIN THE TEXT

1 H. Payne, 'Early Greek Vases from Knossos,' *Annual Brit. School Athens* 29, 1927–28, 240 B 38 Pls. 10–13.—Kunze 76, 3.—C. Weickert, 'Eine geometrische Darstellung aus der Odyssee?' *Röm. Mitt.* 60/61, 1953–54, 57, 4.

2 E. T. H. Brann, 'A Figured Geometric Fragment from the Athenian Agora,' *Antike Kunst*, 2, 1959, 35 Pl. 17, 1.—E. T. H. Brann, 'Late Geometric and Protoattic Pottery,' *The Athenian Agora* 8, 1962 No. 311, Pl. 18.

3 M. Robertson, 'Excavations in Ithaka V,' *Annual Brit. School Athens* 43, 1948, 40, 163 UD. 42 Fig. 29.—C. Weickert, 'Eine geometrische Darstellung aus der Odysee?' *Röm. Mitt.* 60/61, 1953–54, 56ff.—Dunbabin 78, 1.

4 H. Payne, *Protokorinth. Vasenmalerei* (1933) Pl. 11.—E. Buschor, 'Kentauren,' *Amer. Journ. Arch.* 38, 1934, 128ff.—E. Kunze, 'Zum Giebel des Artemistempels in Korfu,' *Athen. Mitt.* 1963.

5 A. Furtwängler, *Olympia* IV (1890) 154 Pl. 59.—E. Pfuhl, *Malerei und Zeichnung* (1923) Fig. 135.—Matz 461 Fig. 34.

6 *Ant. Denkm.* 2 Pl. 52 A 5.— Rumpf *HdA* 34, 2.—J. Dörig, 'Ly ippe und Iphianassa,' *Athen. Mitt.* 77, 1962, 72–91 Appendix 23.

7 Furtwängler *loc. cit.* 463 Pl. 15, 3.—W. Reichel, *Griech. Goldreliefs* (1942) 41a Pl. 13.—Kunze 129ff.—Kunze, Gnomon 1949, 8ff.—Dunbabin 85.

8 A. Furtwängler, *Kleine Schriften* 1 (1911) 458ff. Pl. 15, 1.—W. Reichel, *Griech. Goldreliefs* (1942) 39 No. 37 Pl. 5.—Kunze 228, 1.—Kunze, *Gnomon* 1949, 8ff.

9 K. Friis Johansen, *Les vases sicyoniens* (1923) 92, 9, 143 Pl. 22, 1c.—*CVA* Louvre III Ca Pl. 14,1–4.—H. Payne, *Protokorinth. Vasenmalerei* (1933) Pl. 10,1.—For this and the following vessel cf. G. Beckel, *Götterbeistand* (1961), 97ff.

10 K. Friis Johansen, *Vas. Sicyon.* Pl. 20,1.—*CVA* Oxford II Pl. 1, 5.

11/12 E. Buschor, 'Meermänner,' *Sitzungsberichte Akad. Wiss.* Munich 1941, 14. Fig. 10.—Rumpf 28, 3.

13 R. Eilmann, *CVA* Berlin 1 Pl. 31–33.—Matz 306 Pl. 208.

14 H. L. Lorimer, 'The Hoplite Phalanx,' *Annual Brit. School Athens* 42, 1947, 93 Fig. 7. cf. also *loc. cit.* 100 Fig. 9d.—Dunbabin 78, 2.—Dunbabin *Perachora* II 57, 27 Pl. 2.

15 *Bull. Corr. Hell.* 77, 1953, 265 Fig. 58.—J. M. Cook, *Journ. Hell. Studies* 73, 1953, 116 Fig. 5.

16 G. Rodenwaldt, 'Die Bildwerke des Artemistempels,' *Korkyra* 2 (1939) Pl. 1.—J. Dörig, *Der Kampf der Götter und Titanen* (1961) 33.—K. Schefold, *Griech. Kunst* (1959) 35ff. 62ff.—Riccioni 166.

17   Kunze 82 ff. Pl. 6. Form 1 d.

18   Cf. Pls. 50, 51.

19   P. Jacobsthal, 'Aktaions Tod,' *Marburger Jahrbuch* 5, 1929, 2 Fig. 2.

20   Kunze 78 ff. Pl. 39 Appendix 6, 1/2. Form XIVe.

21   Kunze 78 ff. Pl. 31. Form Xd.—*Enciclopedia dell'arte antica* I (1958) 758 Fig. 955.

22   Kunze 96 ff. Pl. 21. 54. Form. Vd.

23   Payne No. 942 Fig. 45 c.—Kunze 111 ff. A rather earlier and even more impressive version of the Hydra-scene is discussed by G. Beckel in *Götterbeistand* (1961) 42. In this Athene, who has been driving the chariot of Heracles, is accompanied by an owl and a siren and is holding a wine-jug for the approaching victory-celebration with Heracles.

24   Kunze 112 ff. Appendix 7, 4, Form XXIX.

25   Kunze 106 ff. Pl. 30 Form Xa.

26   W. v. Massow, *Athen. Mitt.* 41, 1916, 1 ff. Pl. 10.—E. Simon, 'Arca di Kypselos,' *Enciclopedia dell'arte antica* IV (1961) 427–432.—G. Roux, 'Où avait-on caché le petit Kypsélos?' *Rev. Et. Anc.* 65, 1963, 279–289. For the connection between the pictures see H. Brunn, *Kleine Schriften* 3, 91 ff.: 'When they were representing various scenes in a free association with one another the artists of antiquity had no desire to show themes which were so chronologically close that the one, as it were, should form a continuation of the other. For such close vicinity restricts the scope of possible connections and relationships and encloses them within too narrow bounds ... They preferred either to select moments which were far removed from one another chronologically, and which complemented each other, like beginning and end or cause and effect; or to oppose one scene with a poetical-mythical analogy from a different cycle of legend.'
The picture-books, on the other hand, naturally relate the stories in cyclical form. Traces of such continuous narratives survive even on archaic Etruscan monuments; cf. L. Curtius, *Festschrift Arndt* (1925) 36 ff.

27   Kunze 129 ff. Pl. 21. 54. Form Ve.

28   F. Willemsen, 'Ein früharch. Dreifussbein,' 7th *Olympia-bericht* (1961) 181 ff. Pls. 79–83.

29   P. Orsi, 'Nuove antichità di Gela,' *Mon. Lincei* 19, 1908, 99 Fig. 8.—Kunze 174, 2.—Beazley 53, 49.

30   Pfuhl, *Malerei und Zeichnung* (1923) Fig. 207.—Beazley 97, 22.

31   Kunze 174 ff. Pl. 12. 17 Appendix 13. Inscription: 213, 5.—Vase-painting: E. Simon, *Antike Kunst* 3, 1960, 15 Pl. 6, 1.

32   Kunze 75 ff. Pl. 11, 73. Appendix 6, 3 Form IIf. Variant with inscriptions: E. Kunze, 'Die Ausgrabungen in Olympia 1958–61,' *Deltion* 17, 1961–62, 120 Pl. 137 c.

33   Kunze 165 ff. 170 Pl. 20. 73 Form Vb.

34   Kunze 141 ff. Pl. 42 Form XVb.

35   Kunze 140 ff. Pl. 5. 73 Form Ib.

36   *Monuments Piot* 16, 1908 Pl. 13.—K. Friis Johansen, *Iliaden* (1934) 35 ff. Fig. 6.

37   Payne 135, 10.—K. Friis Johansen, *loc. cit.* 29 ff. Fig. 4.

38   Kunze 149 Pl. 20. 54. Form Vc.

39   W. Fröhner, 'Troianische Vasenbilder,' *Jahrb. d. Inst.* 7, 1892, 28 Pl. 2.—*CVA* III D Pl. 18.—Payne No. 1281.

40   Kunze 157 ff. Pl. 31. 32. 73. Form Xc.

41   Kunze 160 ff. Pl. 26. 29. 27. Form IXc.

42   Kunze 161 ff. Pl. 7. 2. 4. 73. Form Ie.

43   Kunze 167 ff. Pl. 18. 73. Form IVd.

44   Kunze 168 ff. Pl. 6. Form Ic.

45   See note to Pl. 57 c.

46   H. Bulle, 'Odysseus und die Sirenen,' *Strena Helbigiana* (1909) 31 ff.—Payne No. 1282 Pl. 36,5.—Brommer 318 C 1.—A. Fairbanks, *Catalogue of Greek and Etruscan Vases* (1928) 67 No. 467.

I Eleusis, Museum—Height 1.42 m. (56 in.). See note to Pl. 16.

II Syracuse, Museo Archeologico Nazionale.—Height 56 cm. (22 in.). Payne 80 Fig. 23.—S. Benton, 'The Gorgon Plaque at Syracuse,' *Papers Brit. School Rome* 22, 1954, 132–137 Pl. 19, concludes, from the sections for attachment, that Chrysaor was also represented.—H. V. Herrmann, 'Bronzereliefs,' 5th *Olympiabericht* 1956, 91.—*Enciclopedia dell'arte antica* 3 (1960) 984.—Riccioni 163f.—E. Kunze, 'Zum Giebel des Artemistempels in Korfu,' *Athen. Mitt.* 1963.

III Paris, Musée du Louvre E 635.—Height 46 cm. (18$^1/_8$ in.). See note to Pl. 60a.

IV Munich, Staatliche Antikensammlungen, Museum Antiker Kleinkunst 596.—Height 46 cm. (18$^1/_8$ in.). See note to Pl. 66.

V Paris, Musée du Louvre E 640—Height 32 cm. (12$^5/_8$ in.). Payne No. 1473 Pl. 40, 2.—P. E. Arias and M. Hirmer, *A History of Greek Vase Painting* (1962) Pl. 33, XII.—Rumpf 51 Pl. 13, 4.—R .Hampe and E. Simon, *Griech. Sagen* (1964) 23 for other sources of this legend.

VI Athens, National Museum 15499.—Height of the fragment 5.2 cm. (2$^1/_{16}$ in.). Beazley D. 18ff. 107.—Rumpf 39.—Beazley 39, 16.—P. E. Arias and M. Hirmer, *A History of Greek Vase Painting* (1962), Pl. 39.

MONOCHROME PLATES

1 Athens, National Museum 3908—Height 21.5 cm. (8$^1/_2$ in.). F. Matz, *Handbuch der Archäologie* 2 (1954) 208, 5 Pl. 16, 1.—F. Matz, *Kreta, Mykene, Troia* (1957) Pl. 14.—*Enciclopedia dell'arte antica* II (1959) 586 Fig. 800.—For the meaning cf. K. Schefold, *Meisterwerke* (1960) 1ff.—K. Meuli, *Kalewala* (1940).

2a Athens, National Museum 481—Height 22.9 cm. (9 in.). F. Matz, *Kreta, Mykene, Troia* (1957), Pl. 93.—S. Marinatos and M. Hirmer, *Crete and Mycenae* (1960) Pl. 174.—H. G. Buchholz, 'Der Pfeilglätter . . .' *Jahrb. d. Inst.* 77, 1962, 1, 1.

2b Athens, National Museum—Diameter 3.4 cm. (1$^3/_8$ in.). S. Marinatos and M. Hirmer, *Crete and Mycenae* (1960) Pl. 207 bottom.

3a Athens, National Museum—Height of the shoulder-painting approx. 19 cm. (7$^1/_2$ in.). E. Kunze, 'Disiecta Membra att. Grabkratere,' *Ephemeris* 1953–54 (1955) 162ff. Pl. 1.—J. M. Davison, *Attic Geometric Workshops* (1961) 28ff. 135.

3b Brussels, Musée du Cinquantenaire, and Athens, National Museum—Height 28 cm. (11 in.). E. Kunze, 'Bruchstücke attischer Grabkratere, Neue Beiträge,' *Festschrift* B. *Schweitzer* (1952) 48ff.—Davison *loc. cit.* 28, 136 Fig. 16.

4a New York, Metropolitan Museum of Art 17.190.2072—Height 11.3 cm. (4$^7/_{16}$ in.). E. Buschor, 'Kentauren,' *Amer. Journ. Arch.* 38, 1934, 128ff.—Kunze 82ff.—J. Dörig, *Der Kampf der Götter und Titanen* (1961) 37, 5 Pl. 18.—See p. 76 of this work for the oriental legends about the strife between the generations of the gods.—*Enciclopedia dell'arte antica* II (1959) 468 Fig. 650.

4b Olympia, Museum B 1730—Height of surviving section 46.7 cm. (18$^3/_8$ in.). Width of the front 9.5 cm (3$^3/_4$ in.). F. Willemsen, 'Dreifusskessel von Olympia,' *Olymp. Forsch.* III (1957 B 1730 Pl. 63.—Kunze 113ff.—Schäfer 12, 70 Pl. 10, 1.—*Enciclopedia dell'arte antica* III (1960) 378 Fig. 461.

5a Athens, Ceramicus Museum Inv. 407—Height 17.8 cm. (7 in.). K. Kübler, *Kerameikos* V 1, 177.171 No. 4923 Pl. 69.

5b Copenhagen, privately owned, deposited in the Ny Carlsberg Glyptothek—Height 22.5 cm. (8$^7/_8$ in.). V. Poulsen, *Meddelelser fra Ny Carlsberg Glyptothek* 11, 1954 Figs. 4–6.—F. Brommer, *Herakles* (1953) Pl. 18.—For K. F. Johansen's 'Versuch, auf der Kanne Lambros, Aias und Hektor zu erkennen' cf. N. Himmelmann-Wildschütz, *Marburger Winckelmannsprogramm* 1961, 1–5.

5c London, British Museum—Height of the painted strip 9 cm. (3$^1/_2$ in.). Hampe 26, Pl. 22, 1.—Kunze 170, 2.—Hampe G. 30, 18.—W. Kraiker, *Die Malerei der Griechen* (1958) Pl. 5.—Davison *loc. cit.* 67ff. Fig. 98.

6a London, British Museum 3205—Diameter of the rosette approx. 4 cm. (1$^1/_2$ in.). Hampe Pl. 2.—Kunze 102ff.—Schäfer 72, 84.—Cf. fragment of a relief-decorated pithos showing the Wooden Horse: *Praktika* 1949, 131 Fig. 15 and below Pl. 34ff.

6b Athens, National Museum 11765—Height 6 cm (2$^3/_8$ in.). Hampe Pl. 14.—*Enciclopedia dell'arte antica* III (1960) 693, Fig. 780.

6c Munich, Staatliche Münzsammlung A 1293—Width 3.23 cm (1$^1/_4$ in.). G. Kleiner and D. Ohly, 'Gemmen der Sammlung Arndt,' *Münchner Jahrbuch* 1951, 21, 7 Fig. 21 No. A 1293.—J. Boardman, *Island Gems* (1963) does not give the interpretation.

7a Athens, Agora Museum Inv. P 4885—Height 22.8 cm. (9 in.). Hampe 87 Fig. 31.—T. Leslie Shear, 'The Campaign of 1935,' *Hesperia* 5, 1936, 25 Figs. 23, 24.—Kunze 93. 125. 181.

7b Nauplia, Museum—Diameter approx. 40 cm. (15³/₄ in.). D. v. Bothmer, *Amazons in Greek Art* (1957), Pl. I 1a–b.— K. Schefold, *Griechische Kunst* (1959) Pl. 2 (Interpretation).

8 Munich, Staatliche Antikensammlungen, Museum Antiker Kleinkunst 8696—Height 21.5 cm. (8¹/₂ in.). *Enciclopedia dell'arte antica* III (1960) 826 Fig. 1024.—Hampe G. 27, Pl. 7, 8.

9 Naxos, Museum—Height of the illustrated section 19 cm· (7¹/₂ in.). C. Karusos, 'Eine naxische Amphora des frühen 7. Jh.', *Jahrbuch des Inst.* 52, 1937, 166ff.—Rumpf 38 Pl. 6, 6.—*Enciclopedia dell'arte antica* I (1958) 115 Fig. 169.

10 Athens, National Museum 3961.911—Height 95 cm. (37³/₈ in.). E. Buschor, *Griechische Vasen* (1940) Fig. 66.—P. E. Arias and M. Hirmer, *A History of Greek Vase Painting* (1962) 29 Pl. 22.—P. E. Arias, *Enciclopedia dell'arte antica* II (1959) 598 Fig. 805.—R. Hampe and E. Simon, *Griech. Sagen* (1964) 59, 33.

11a Athens, National Museum—Height 7.3 cm. (2⁷/₈ in.), R. M. Dawkins, *Artemis Orthia* (1929) 209 Pl. 100.—Kunze. *Gnomon* 1933, 14.—Kunze 91ff.

11b Paris, Bibliothèque Nationale—Height 25 cm. (9⁷/₈ in.). A. de Ridder, *Catalogue des vases peints de la Bibliothèque Nationale* (1902) Pl. 34, 166.—Schäfer 73 B 5. 82ff.

12 Athens, National Museum 5898—Height 1.20 m. (47¹/₄ in.). E. Buschor, *Plastik der Griechen* (1936) 14.—Schäfer 73 B 1. 81ff.

13 Tenos, Museum. *Praktika* 1953, 264ff. Fig. 9.—N. M. Kontoleon, *Atti del settimo congresso di Arch.* 1, 262ff.—*Amer. Journ. Arch.* 58, 1954 Pl. 46, Fig. 13.—*Bull. Corr. Hell.* 78, 1954, 145.— N. M. Kontoleon, whom I should like, at this point, to thank for permission to use the illustration, is shortly to publish the pithos in the *Archaiologike Ephemeris* (also 'Η γέννησις τοῦ Διός, *Kretika Chronika* 1963, 283ff. Fig. NB.).—F. Brommer, 'Die Geburt der Athena,' *Jb. Mainz* 8, 1961, 72, thinks the enthroned figure may represent Metis.

14 New York, Metropolitan Museum of Art 17. 190.73— Height 13.7 cm. (5³/₈ in.). G. M. A. Richter 'An Ivory Relief,' *Amer. Journ. Arch.* 49, 1945, 261.—G. M. A. Richter, *Handbook* (1953) 180a, Pl. 20.—F. Matz, 'Arge und Opis,' *Marburger Winckelmannsprogramm* 1948, 3ff.—On the subject of Zeus' seduction on Mt Ida cf. P. Von der Mühll, *Hypomnema* 222ff.— J. Dörig, 'Lysippe und Iphianassa,' *Athen. Mitt.* 77, 1962, 72ff. (interpretation as the Proitides, cf. Fig. 6.

15a Heraklion, Museum—Height 14.4 cm. (5¹¹/₁₆ in.). D. Levi, *Annuario Atene* 13/14, 1933, Pl. 14ff.—M. Guarducci, *Riv. Ist.*

Arch. 6, 1937, 7ff.—S. Benton, 'The Dating of Helmets and Corselets in Early Greece,' *Annual Brit. School Athens* 40, 1939–40, 78ff. Pl. 28.—D. Levi, 'Gleanings from Crete,' *Amer. Journ. Arch.* 49, 1945, 293ff. Fig. 15.—Matz Pl. 272a.—C. Picard, *Studies . . . Robinson* 1, 1951, 655ff.—N. M. Kontoleon, 'Η γέννησις τοῦ Διός, *Kretika Chronika* 1963, 263ff.

15b Paris, Musée du Louvre CA 795—Total height 1.30 m. (51¹/₄ in.). Hampe 56 Pl. 36–38.—Schäfer 73 B 2.—Kunze 136ff.— *Enciclopedia dell'arte antica* III (1960) 981 Fig. 1254.—On the subject of the presumed Perseus-poetry cf. G. Beckel, *Götterbeistand* (1961) 40.—Riccioni 146.

16 Eleusis, Museum—Height 1.42 m. (56 in.). G. E. Mylonas 'Ο πρωτοαττικὸς 'αμφορὸς τῆς 'Ελευσῖνος (1957), 134 Pl. 16, 2.—P. E. Arias and M. Hirmer, *A History of Greek Vase Painting* (1962) Pls. 12, 13.—Riccioni 153—155.

17 Vathy, Samos, Museum—Height approx. 10 cm. (4 in.). R. Hampe, 'Korfugiebel und frühe Perseusbilder,' *Athen. Mitt.* 60/61, 1935/36, 288, Pl. 99, 2.—Matz Pl. 233b.—G. Beckel, *Götterbeistand* (1961) 36.—Riccioni 165.

18 Athens, National Museum—Approx. 80 × 80 cm. (31¹/₂ × 31¹/₂ in.). H. Payne, *Annual Brit. School Athens* 27, 1925–26, 124.—R. Hampe, 'Korfugiebel und frühe Perseusbilder,' *Athen. Mitt.* 60/61, 1935–36, 293, 13.—Kunze 136ff.—Rumpf 34 Pl. 8, 1.—K. Schauenburg, *Perseus* (1960) Note 201.—W. Kraiker, *Die Malerei der Griechen* (1958) Pl. II.

19 Athens, National Museum—Approx. 80 × 80 cm. (31¹/₂ × 31¹/₂ in.). *Ant. Denkm.* 2, Pl. 52.—Rumpf 34, 2.

20 Athens, National Museum—Approx. 80 × 80 cm. (31¹/₂ × 31¹/₂ in.). *Ant. Denkm.* 2, Pl. 50, 1.—Rumpf 34, 2.—M. Robertson, *Griech. Malerei* (1959) 50.

21 Athens, National Museum—Height approx. 88 cm. (34¹/₂ in.). *Ant. Denkm.* 2 Pl. 51, 2.—Rumpf 34, 2 Pl. 8, 2.—W. Kraiker. *Die Malerei der Griechen* (1958) Pl. 13.

22 Aegina, Museum—Height approx. 17 cm. (6³/₄ in.). W. Kraiker, *Aigina* (1951) No. 253, Pl. 18.—*Enciclopedia dell'arte antica* II (1959) 45 Fig. 77.—Early Cretan paintings: D. Levi, 'Gli scavi sull'Acropoli di Gortina,' *Annuario Atene N. S.* 17/18, 1955–56, 274 Figs. 57, 62.

23 New York, Metropolitan Museum of Art 11.210.1—Height 1.09 m. (42⁷/₈ in.). Kunze 93ff.—G. M. A. Richter, *Handbook* (1953) Pl. 187b.—K. Schefold, 'Drei archaische Dichtungen von Herakles,' *Mus. Helv.* 19, 1962, 131.—S. G. Kapsomenos, *Sophokles' Trachinierinnen und ihr Vorbild* (1963).—On the owl, cf. G. Beckel, *Götterbeistand* (1961) 46. 42.—J. H. Jonkees, *Mnemosyne* 1952, 28.—F. Brommer, *Jahrb. Berl. Mus.* 1962, 1ff.

24a Berlin, Staatliche Museen, Antikensammlung F 336— Height 6.5 cm. ($2^9/_{16}$ in.). H. Payne, *Protokorinth. Vasenmalerei* Pl. 21, 1–4.—Brommer 69 C 1.

24b Sparta, Museum—Height 7.7 cm. (3 in.). R. M. Dawkins, *Artemis Orthia* (1929) 209 Pl. 101.—Matz Pl. 233a.—E. Kunze, *Gnomon* 1933, 14.

24c Mykonos, Museum—Height 38.2 cm. (15 in.). C. Dugas, *Delos* 17, 1935 Pl. 12/3 No. 19.—For the interpretation cf. *Eur. El.* 442ff.—*Iph. Aul.* 1071ff.—F. Friedländer, *Johannes von Gaza* (1912) 26, 1.—P. Von der Mühll, *Hypomnema* (1952) 281, 43 and, particularly, K. Friis Johansen, *Iliaden* (1934) 52ff.

25a Basle, Antikenmuseum—Height 1.55 m. (61 in.). E. Berger, *Cibablätter*, July/August 1962.—Other scholars (*e. g.* F. Eckstein, *Atlantis* 1964, 169) see the last girl on the top frieze as Ariadne.

25b Boston, Museum of Fine Arts 528—Height 1.57 m. ($61^3/_4$ in.), diameter 81 cm. ($31^7/_8$ in.). A. Fairbanks, *Boston Cat.* (1928) Pl. 52.—Hampe 56 Pl. 39.

26 Olympia, Museum—Height 40 cm. ($15^3/_4$ in.). Unpublished.

27a Privately owned—Height 9.5 cm. ($3^3/_4$ in.). E. Langlotz, 'Ein Votivrelief aus Tarent,' *Festschrift Amelung* (1928) 113.— Matz I Pl. 140b.

27b Heraklion, Museum—Height 32 cm. ($12^5/_8$ in.). E. Buschor, *Griech. Vasen* (1940) Fig. 56.—D. Levi, 'Arkades,' *Annuario Atene* 10/12, 1927–29, 338, Fig. 443a–d, Pl. 23.—Rumpf Pl. 4, 7.—W. Kraiker, *Die Malerei der Griechen* (1958) Pl. 9 top.— *Enciclopedia dell'arte antica* I (1958) 659 Fig. 842.

27c Olympia, Museum—Width 33 cm. (13 in.). R. Hampe, 1st *Olympiabericht* (1937) 85ff., Pl. 28.—E. Kunze, *Neue Meisterwerke* (1948) No. 36.—Matz Pl. 283b.—*Enciclopedia dell'arte antica* II (1959) 469 Fig. 451.—K. Schauenburg, 'Eine neue Sianaschale,' *Arch. Anz.* 1962, 747ff., for Caeneus-paintings.

28 Athens, National Museum—Height 19 cm. ($7^1/_2$ in.). J. Martha, *Cat. terr. cuit. d'Athènes* (1880) No. 559.—P. Jacobsthal, *Die melischen Reliefs* (1931) 91 Pl. 68.

29a Berlin-Charlottenburg, Staatliche Museen, Antikenabteilung Inv. 31573 A 9—Height of the neck 17.5 cm. ($6^7/_8$ in.). R. Eilmann *CVA* Berlin 1 Pl. 5.—E. Buschor, *Griech. Vasen* (1940) Fig. 45.—Matz I, Pl. 215.

29b Rome, Villa Giulia—Height of the vase 26 cm. ($10^1/_4$ in.). *Ant. Denkm.* 2, 1899–1901 Pl. 44f.—P. E. Arias and M. Hirmer, *A History of Greek Vase Painting*, (1962), 276 Pls. 16, 17, IV.

29c Basle, privately owned—Height approx. 6.2 cm. ($2^1/_2$ in.). J. L. Benson, *Die Geschichte der korinthischen Vasen* (1953) Pl. 2.— K. Schefold, *Meisterwerke* (1960) No. 82.

30, 31 Boston, Museum of Fine Arts 529—Height 1.10 m. ($43^1/_4$ in.), diameter 68 cm. ($26^3/_4$ in.). A. Fairbanks, *Boston Cat.* (1928) Pl. 53.—Hampe Pls. 36, 37.—Matz Pl. 253.

32a New York, Metropolitan Museum of Art 42. 11. 13— Diameter 1.9 cm. ($3/_4$ in.). G. M. A. Richter, *Catalogue of Engraved Gems* (1956) No. 13 Pl. 3.

32b Naples, Museo Nazionale Archeologico—Height 17 cm. ($6^{11}/_{16}$ in.). Hampe Pl. 35.—A. Levi, *Le terracotte figurate del Mus. Naz. di Napoli* (1926) 170. 766 Fig. 130.—Matz I Pl. 279b.

32c Athens, National Museum—Height 46.3 cm. ($18^1/_4$ in.). Hampe Pl. 41.—Matz Pl. 292b.—*Enciclopedia dell'arte antica* II (1959) 721 Fig. 956.

33 Heraklion, Museum—Height 8.5 cm. ($3^3/_8$ in.). D. Levi, *Annuario Atene* 33/34, 1955–56, 260 Fig. 56.

34 35a–b Mykonos, Museum—Height of 34: 1.34 m. ($52^3/_4$ in.); height of 35a: 15 cm. ($5^{15}/_{16}$ in.). M. Ervin, 'A Relief Pithos from Mykonos,' *Deltion* 18, 1961–62 (1964).—G. Daux, *Bull. Corr. Hell.* 86, 1962, 855 Fig. 16 Pl. 29.—H. Walter, 'Amazonen oder Achäer?' *Athen. Mitt.* 77, 1962, 195ff.

36a Berlin-Charlottenburg, Staatliche Museen, Antikenabteilung A 31—Height 66 cm. (26 in.). R. Eilmann *CVA* 1 Pl. 18ff.— Buschor, *Griech. Vasen* Fig. 46.—Matz Pls. 210, 211.—Kunze 169.—For the mitra, in Olympia, mentioned in the text, cf. E. Kunze, 'Die Ausgrabungen in Olympia 1958–1961,' *Deltion* 17, 1961–62, 118.

36b Boston, Museum of Fine Arts 528—Height 1.57 m. ($61^3/_4$ in.). A. Fairbanks, *Boston Cat.* (1928) Pl. 52.—Hampe Pl. 38.—Kunze 157, 3.169.

37 Aegina, Museum—Diameter of belly of vase 25.5 cm. (10 in.). W. Kraiker, *Aigina, Die Vasen des 10. bis 7. Jh.* (1951) No. 566 Pl. 44/45.—Rumpf 25 Pl. 4, 3.—K. Kübler, *Altattische Malerei* (1950) 60 Fig. 51.

38 Delphi, Museum Inv. 467 and 980; 1524—Height without stand 2.16 and 2.18 m. (85 and 86 in.) respectively. R. Lullies and M. Hirmer, *Greek Sculpture* 2nd ed. (1960) Pls. 14, 15.

39 Missing—Height 19.1 cm. ($7^1/_2$ in.). D. Ohly, *Athen. Mitt.* 68, 1953, 77 Appendix 13–15, 18–19.—*Enciclopedia dell'arte antica* III (1960) 1144, 1462.—E. Buschor, *Altsamische Standbilder* 4 (1960) Fig. 250.

40a Athens, National Museum 16.285—Height 32 cm. ($12^5/_8$ in.). S. Karusu, *Annuario Atene* 24–26, 1950, 37ff.—Beazley 19, 3.— B. F. Cook, *Bull. Metrop. Mus. New York* 1962, 31.

40b Athens, Ceramicus Museum Inv. 154—Height of the painted section 18.5 cm. ($7^5/_{16}$ in.). D. Ohly, 'Die Chimären des Chimäramalers,' *Athen. Mitt.* 76, 1961, 1ff.—Beazley 3, 3.

41a Olympia, Museum—Height approx. 20 cm. ($7^7/_8$ in.). E. Kunze, 'Die Ausgrabungen in Olympia 1958–1961,' *Deltion* 17, 1961–62, 120 Pl. 137a.—There is a better preserved representation of the relief in Kunze 39 No. 63 Pl. 68.

41b Athens, Acropolis Museum 631—Height approx. 12 cm. ($4^3/_4$ in.). Beazley 108, 6.—J. Dörig, *Der Kampf der Götter und Titanen* (1961) 18 Pl. 8b.— Otherwise R. Hampe *GGA* 1963, 137.

42, 43 Corfu, Museum—Height 2.60 m. (102 in.). Kunze 88ff.— G. Rodenwaldt, *Die Bildwerke des Artemistempels von Korkyra* (1939) Pl. 25–28.—K. Schefold, *Orient, Hellas und Rom* (1949) 96ff.—Riccioni 166ff.—J. Dörig, *Der Kampf der Götter und Titanen* (1961).—R. Hampe *GGA* 1963, 125–152.—E. Kunze, 'Zum Giebel des Artemistempels in Korfu,' *Athen. Mitt.* 1963.

44a Berlin-Charlottenburg, Staatliche Museen, Antikenabteilung F 1682—Height 21.5 cm. ($8^7/_{16}$ in.). *CVA* Berlin 1 Pl. 46ff.— Beazley D. 15, 10 Pl. 5, 2.—K. Schauenburg, *Perseus* 94.224.— Beazley 5, 4.

44b Berlin, Staatliche Museen, Antikensammlung F 1652— Height 35 cm. ($13^3/_4$ in.). Payne No. 1431.—Brommer 216.— Kunze 138.—*Enciclopedia dell'arte antica* I (1958) 363 Fig. 503.— K. Kerényi, *Heroen* (1958) Fig. 7.—S. Morenz, 'Die orientalische Herkunft der Perseus-Andromedasage,' *Forsch. und Fortschr.* 36, 1962, 307–309.

45 Paris, Musée du Louvre E 874—Total height 93 cm. ($36^5/_8$ in.). Beazley D. 16ff.—P. E. Arias and M. Hirmer, *A History of Greek Vase Painting* (1962) Pls. 35–37.—I. Scheibler, 'Olpen und Amphoren des Gorgomalers,' *Jahrb. d. Inst.* 76, 1961, 6ff.— Beazley 8, 1.—*Enciclopedia dell'arte antica* III (1960) 985 Fig. 1261.— Riccioni 171.

46–52 Florence, Museo Archeologico 4209—Height 66 cm. (26 in.). A. Furtwängler and K. Reichhold, *Griech. Vasenmalerei*, Pls. 1–3. 11–13.—Beazley 76, 1.—Beazley D. 26ff. 108ff. Pl. 11.— P. E. Arias and M. Hirmer, *A History of Greek Vase Painting* (1962) Pls. 40–46.—A. Minto, *Il Vaso François* (1960).—*Enciclopedia dell'arte antica* IV (1961) 366ff. Figs. 433–4.—On the subject of the archers, cf. J. Wiesner, *Mitt. Anthrop. Ges. Wien* 92, 1962, 295.—R. Hampe and E. Simon in *Griech. Sagen* (1964) 65, have indicated a somewhat later Etruscan Achilles-cycle on the bronze chariot from Monteleone.

53 Hamburg, Museum für Kunst und Gewerbe Inv. 1960.1— Height 41.5 cm. ($16^5/_{16}$ in.). H. Hoffmann, *Kunst und Altertum in Hamburg* (1961) 60.—Cf. also the Tyrrhenian amphora Tarquinia (*Ant. Denkm.* 1 Pl. 22) which, with G. Loeschke, *Jahrb. d. Inst.* 2, 1887, 275ff., and Buschor in *Furtwängler-Reichhold* 3, 282, I would be more inclined to associate with the Niobids than with Tityos (as does Beazley 97, 32.).

54a Athens, Acropolis Museum 1—Width 5.80 m. (228 in.), height 79 cm. ($31^1/_8$ in.). Lippold 36, 1.—Schefold, *Griech. Pla-*

stik I (1949) 24ff. 37 Pl. 21.—On the subject of the Heracles representations, cf. also Kunze 104ff., 115 (the boar and struggle for the tripod are High Archaic).—*Enciclopedia dell'arte antica* I (1958) 782 Fig. 982.

54b Rome, Villa Giulia—Height 36 cm. ($14^3/_{16}$ in.). K. Schefold, *Griech. Kunst* (1959) Pl. 6a.—Beazley 121, 6.

54c Paris, Musée du Louvre CA 3004—Height 12 cm. ($4^3/_4$ in.). *Brommer* 65, 6.—R. Amandry, 'Skyphos corinthien du Musée du Louvre,' *Mon. Piot.* 40, 1944 Pl. 3. 4.

55a Vathy, Samos, Museum—Beazley D. 21, Pl. 7, 1.—Beazley 25, 18.

55b Delphi, Museum—Height 58 cm. ($22^7/_8$ in.). P. de la Coste-Messelière, *Au Musée de Delphes* (1936) 153ff.—Lippold 24, 8.

56 Athens, Acropolis Museum—Width of both sections together 16.16 m. (636 in.), height 1.70 m. (67 in.). W.-H. Schuchhardt, 'Die Sima des alten Athenatempels der Akropolis,' *Athen. Mitt.* 60/1, 1935–36, 65ff.—Lippold 36 Pl. 6, 2. 8, 3.—K. Schefold, *Griech. Plastik* I (1949) Pls. 24–26.—*Enciclopedia dell'arte antica* I (1958) 778/9 Figs. 977–979.—R. Lullies and M. Hirmer, *Greek Sculpture* 2nd ed. (1960) Pls. 26 and I, II.

57a Athens, National Museum 16384—Height of body of krater 34.5 cm. ($13^9/_{16}$ in.). Kunze, 92, 1.—Brommer 140, 2.— Beazley 6.—S. Karusu, *Angeia tou Anagyrountos* (1963) 11ff. Pls. 21ff.

57b Olympia, Museum—Width of strip 6.8 cm. ($2^{11}/_{16}$ in.). Kunze 121ff., 170ff. Form III Pl. 15.—J. Dörig, *Der Kampf der Götter und Titanen* (1961) 17ff.

57c Athens, National Museum 354—Height 1 m. ($39^1/_2$ in.). Buschor, *Griech. Vasen* (1940) Fig. 67.—Rumpf 44, 1.—W. Kraiker, *Die Malerei der Griechen* (1958) 151, 11, Pl. 11.—*Enciclopedia dell'arte antica* II (1959) Fig. 808.

58a Cambridge, Fitzwilliam Museum 44—Height of the vessel 38 cm. (15 in.). Beazley 84, 2.—*CVA* Cambridge 1, III HE Pl. 8, 2.—D. v. Bothmer, 'The Camtar Painter,' *Antike Kunst* 2, 1959, 6 Pl. 3, 1.—Bothmer, *Amazons in Greek Art* (1957) 6. 135 Pl. 2, 2.

58b Brussels, Musée du Cinquantenaire A 1374—Height 10.7 cm. ($4^3/_{16}$ in.). Payne No. 986 Pl. 34, 6.—*CVA* Brussels 1 Pl. 4, 2a.—Brommer 2 C 1.

58c Gela, Antiquario—Height 14.3 cm. ($5^5/_8$ in.). M. I. Wiencke, 'An Epic Theme in Greek Art,' *Amer. Journ. Arch.* 58, 1954, 292ff. Pl. 56 Fig. 4.—E. T. H. Brann, 'A Figured Geometric Fragment,' *Antike Kunst* 2, 1959, 37 Pl. 17, 2.

59 Athens, National Museum 1002—Height 1.22 m. (48 in.). P. E. Arias and M. Hirmer, *A History of Greek Vase Painting* (1962) 18–20.—On the subject of the theme, cf. K. Schauenburg, *Perseus* (1960).—And finally F. G. Lo Porto, 'Ceramica arcaica della necr. di Taranto,' *Annuario Atene* 1959–60, 210.—Riccioni 170.

60a Paris, Musée du Louvre E 635—Height 46 cm. (18^1/$_8$ in.). Payne No. 780 Pl. 27.—P. E. Arias and M. Hirmer, *A History of Greek Vase Painting* (1962) Pls. 32 and IX.—K. Schefold, 'Drei archaische Dichtungen von Herakles,' *Mus. Helv.* 19, 1962, 131ff.—*Enciclopedia dell'arte antica* I (1958) 846 Fig. 1110.

60b Privately owned—Height 8.5 cm. (3^3/$_8$ in.). R. Blatter, 'Dinosfragmente mit der kalydonischen Eberjagd,' *Antike Kunst* 5, 1962, 45ff. Pl. 16.

61a Olympia, Museum Inv. B 2198—Width of the strip 8.1 cm. (3^3/$_{16}$ in.). Kunze 117ff. XXIXa Pl. 56.

61b Privately owned—Height 19 cm. (7^1/$_2$ in.). R. Blatter, 'Dinosfragmente mit der kalydonischen Eberjagd,' *Antike Kunst* 5, 1962, 45ff. Pl. 16.

62 Paris, Musée du Louvre L 173—Height 10 cm. (3^{15}/$_{16}$ in.). P. V. C. Baur, *Centaurs in Ancient Art* (1912) 94 Fig. 21.—Payne No. 941 Pl. 31, 9–10.—Brommer 138 C 1.—G. Beckel, *Götterbeistand* (1961) 45. (If the centaurs were about to attack the gods, as Beckel thinks, the gods would be behaving differently!)

63a–b Delphi Museum—Height of each 58 cm. (22^7/$_8$ in.).

63a P. de la Coste-Messelière, *Au Musée de Delphes* (1936) 177ff. For the metope fragment with Phrixus on the ram cf. *l oc. cit.* Pl. 1 E.—For Phrixus on Acropolis fragment cf. I. Scheibler, *Jahrb. d. Inst.* 76, 1961, 30, 86.

63b P. de la Coste-Messelière, *Au Musée de Delphes* (1936) 199ff. Pl. 15.—Lippold 24ff. 8.

64a Berlin-Charlottenburg, Staatliche Museen, Antikenabteilung F 1682—Height 21.5 cm. (8^7/$_{16}$ in.). See note to Pl. 44a.

64b Delphi, Museum—Height 9 cm. (3^9/$_{16}$ in.). P. Amandry, 'Rapport préliminaire sur les statues chryséléphantines de Delphes,' *Bull. Corr. Hell.* 63, 1939, 86ff.—P. Amandry, *Bull. Corr. Hell.* 64, 1940–41, 271.—*Enciclopedia dell'arte antica* IV (1961) 430 Fig. 500.

65 Athens, National Museum—Largest diameter 76 cm. (30 in.). Graef-Langlotz, *Die antiken Vasen von der Akropolis zu Athen* I (1909) 64–65 Pl. 27.—C. Roebuck, 'Fragments Joining Vases from the Acropolis,' *Hesperia* 9, 1940, 146 Fig. 1.

66 Munich, Staatliche Antikensammlungen, Museum Antiker Kleinkunst 596—Height 46 cm. (18^1/$_8$ in.). A. Rumpf, *Chalkidische Vasen* (1927) 12 Pl. 23–25.—P. E. Arias and M. Hirmer, *A History of Greek Vase Painting* (1962), Pl. XXV.—*Enciclopedia dell'arte antica* I (1958) Fig. 950.

67a Previously in Berlin, Staatliche Museen F 1655—Total height 46 cm. (18^1/$_8$ in.). Now missing. Furtwängler-Reichhold, *Griech. Vasenmalerei* Pl. 121.—Payne No. 1471.—E. Buschor, *Griech. Vasen* (1940) Figs. 81–82.—*Enciclopedia dell'arte antica* I (1958) 371 Fig. 518.

67b Florence, Museo Archeologico 70995—Height 36.3 cm. (14^1/$_4$ in.). Pfuhl, *Malerei und Zeichnung* (1923) Fig. 211.—Beazley 110, 32.

68, 69 Sparta, Museum—Height 67 cm. (26^3/$_8$ in.). M. N. Tod and A. J. B. Wace, *Catalogue of the Sparta Museum* (1906) 132, 1.—Kunze 164.—L. Ghali-Kahil, *Les enlèvements et le retour d'Hélène* (1955) 71, 24.—C. A. Christos, *Ephemeris* 1955, 95. Fig. 4.

70a New York, Metropolitan Museum of Art 27.116—Tota height 40.6 cm. (16 in.). Payne No. 1187.—L. Ghali-Kahil, *Les enlèvements et le retour d'Hélène* (1955) 117. 112 Pl. 40, 1.

70b–c Paris, Musée du Louvre E 639—Height 39 cm. (15^3/$_8$ in.). Payne No. 1461.—Brommer 248 C 1.

71a Boston, Museum of Fine Arts 2121—Total height 37 cm. (14^9/$_{16}$ in.). Beazley 84, 3.—D. v. Bothmer, 'The Camtar Painter,' *Antike Kunst* 2, 1959, Pl. 2.

71b Paris, Musée du Louvre E 638—Total height 42.5 cm. (16^3/$_4$ in.). Payne No. 1474.

72 Naples, Astarita Collection—Height 47.3 cm. (18^5/$_8$ in.). J. D. Beazley, *Proceedings of the British Academy* (1957) 233ff. Pls. 11–16.—*Enciclopedia dell'arte antica* II (1959), coloured plate opposite 848.

73a Munich, Staatliche Antikensammlungen, Museum Antiker Kleinkunst 1426 (J. 124)—Height 40 cm. (15^3/$_4$ in.). Beazley 95, 5.—Buschor, *Griech. Vasen* (1940) 107 Fig. 123.—H. V. Herrmann, *Der Omphalos* (1959).—*Rev. Gnomon* 1960, 258.—*Amer. Journ. Arch.* 1963, 102.—On the subject of Troilus-representations cf. K. Schauenburg, 'Achilleus in der unterital. Vasenmalerei,' *Bonner Jb.* 161, 1961, 219, 22, 23.

73b Brussels, Musée du Cinquantenaire—Height 27.8 cm. (11 in.). *CVA* Brussels 1, Pl. 5, 2a/b.—Pfuhl, *Malerei und Zeichnung* (1923), Fig. 175.—Payne 136 No. 1410; *Inscription* 165, 38.

74 Vatican Museums 125—Height 30.3 cm. (12 in.). Payne 165, 35 No. 1396.—Brommer 279 C 3.—K. Friis Johansen, *Iliaden i tidlig graesk kunst* (1934) 147, 5 Fig. 5.

75 London, British Museum A 749—Diameter 38.5 cm. (15^1/$_8$ in.). P. E. Arias and M. Hirmer, *A History of Greek Vase Painting* (1962) Pl. 27.—Rumpf 36 Pl. 7, 4.—Matz Pl. 183.

76a Olympia, Museum Inv. B 974 a. b—Height 9.9 cm. (3⁷/₈ in.). E. Kunze, 3rd *Olympiabericht* (1938–39) 96ff. Pl. 31.

76b Berlin-Charlottenburg, Staatliche Museen, Antikenabteilung 8099—Height 5 cm. (2 in.). Kunze 145ff. Appendix 11.

76c Berlin, Staatliche Museen, Antikensammlung 1147—Height 33 cm. (13 in.). Payne No. 1170.—Brommer 260 C 1.—*Enciclopedia dell'arte antica* IV (1961) 999 Fig. 1189.

77 Delphi, Museum 4479—Width of strip 6.2 cm. (2⁷/₁₆ in.). *Fouilles de Delphes* V 123 Pl. 21.—Kunze 25, 38 Pl. 50.

78a Paris, Musée du Louvre E 635—Total height 46 cm. (18¹/₈ in.). See note to plate 60a.

78b Naples, Museo Nazionale Archeologico—Diameter 36 cm. (14³/₁₆ in.). E. Gabrici, *Röm. Mitt.* 27, 1912, Pls. 5, 6.—E. Gabrici *Mon. Linc.* 22, 1914 Pl. 57.—Hampe 85.—Kunze 159ff.—Beazley D. 24ff. (lower Pl. 10).—Cf. also M. I. Wiencke, 'An Epic Theme in Greek Art,' *Amer. Journ. Arch.* 58, 1954, 293ff.

79 Paris, Musée du Louvre E 643—Height 45 cm. (17³/₄ in.). Payne No. 1446 Pl. 37, 7.—M. Wegner, *Meisterwerke der Griechen* (1955) 85.

80 Olympia, Museum. G. Daux, 'Chronique des fouilles,' *Bull. Corr. Hell.* 84, 1960, 720 Pl. 18, 2.

Addendum:

Hampe 42ff., and K. Meuli, *Schweiz. Archiv. f. Volkskunde* 56, 1960, 125–139, have identified Heracles' hunt of the horned Ceryneian hind on a Boeotian bronze fibula of *c.* 700 BC. The Greeks had forgotten the original meaning of this legend and could now only express admiration for the long duration of the pursuit which lasted an entire year. Meuli believes the original meaning of the legend to be that the hero was making accessible to men one of the miraculous creatures of a primeval age; in many illustrations he is actually breaking off the hind's antlers. Such legends which tell of heroes who, by a heroic deed, make 'the terrifyingly powerful world of primeval ages a place for men to live in and use' are widespread.

12/12/66